The Healing
Presence

The Healing Presence

Spiritual Exercises for Healing, Wellness, and Recovery

THOMAS A. DROEGE

HarperSanFrancisco
A Division of HarperCollins*Publishers*

Library of Congress Cataloging-in-Publication Data

Droege, Thomas A. (Thomas Arthur).
   The healing presence : spiritual exercises for healing, wellness,
and recovery / Thomas A. Droege.
     p.   cm.
   ISBN 0-06-062097-8 (alk. paper)
    1. Spiritual exercises. 2. Spiritual healing.   3. Imagination—
Religious aspects—Christianity.   I. Title
BV4509.5.D76   1992
248.3'4—dc20   91-50499
                                              CIP

92 93 94 95 96 RRD(H) 10 9 8 7 6 5 4 3 2 1
This edition is printed on acid-free paper that meets the American
National Standards Institute Z39.48 Standard.

*To Robert Perry from whom I learned
the power of imagery in spiritual direction*

Contents

Preface

In your mind's eye picture a bright yellow lemon in your hand. In your other hand take a sharp knife and cut a wedge out of the lemon. As you take that wedge in your hand, notice how yellow the lemon is and how glistening drops of juice have formed on the edges of the fruit. Sniff its fragrance and then place the wedge in your mouth, sinking your teeth into its tender pulp. Experience the tartness as your mouth puckers up.

That's guided imagery. It's using your imagination to experience something that you've done before or can imagine doing now or will be doing in the future. If you took the time to do what I suggested above and really did imagine taking a bite out of a lemon, it's likely that the flow of saliva in your mouth increased and your lips puckered up. To say that something is a figment of the imagination means that it's not real. Your body responds to the use of imagery as if it were real, as if the experience were actually happening.

That's why I am convinced that imagery is such a powerful tool for facilitating healing and maintaining wellness. It's one of the best means we have for both giving and receiving information from our bodies. Imagery is a deeper-than-intellectual consciousness that is already widely used in medicine for inducing relaxation, for biofeedback, and for control of pain. The more active the imagination and the deeper the experience, the more effective is the imagery. For example, during the intermission of the film *Lawrence of Arabia,* the desert classic, concession stands were inundated with requests for drinks, so immersed were viewers in the hot, sandy story they were seeing.

Though a powerful tool for facilitating healing and maintaining wellness, imagery is not a substitute for medical interventions or psychiatric care. The use of imagery in healing complements the practice of medicine. Healing in both realms is self-healing in the sense that the human body has a wondrous capacity to heal itself. Both medicine and the use of healing imagery in the church facilitate that process of healing, one by physical means and the other by spiritual means. In both cases, Christians insist, the ultimate source of healing is God.

"Guided" imagery means that someone functions as a guide to your imagination. You need only allow yourself to experience what the guide is suggesting. After inducing a state of relaxation, perhaps by asking you to imagine yourself in a place that is peaceful and quiet, a guide may suggest that you recall some event in the past, not necessarily one where you were present. With the aid of an effective guide, that experience can become so real that it is as if it were happening. You can learn to be your own guide, as you will see in chapter 1.

The use of imagery by Christians is a natural outgrowth of the rich use of images in Scripture, making it an appropriate tool for deepening the experience of faith. Faith, in turn, is a factor in healing, as is abundantly clear in the healing stories of Jesus.* The exercises in this volume are designed to deepen the experience of faith as that relates to healing.

Completion of this project was made possible by a sabbatical leave from Valparaiso University and appointment as university research professor, supplemented by the O. P. Kretzmann Memorial Scholarship, which is awarded annually to a member of the Valparaiso University faculty for study in the healing arts and is funded by the Wheat Ridge Foundation.

---

*In a recent book I have shown that faith is always a factor in healing, wherever and by whomever it is done. Focusing particularly on medical healing, I examined the faith factor in the placebo effect, the stories of illness, and the use of imagery. See Thomas A. Droege, *The Faith Factor in Healing* (Philadelphia: Trinity Press International, 1991).

I wish to pay tribute to the congregations in the San Francisco Bay area, where I field-tested the exercises in this guidebook. They responded enthusiastically to my request for permission to test these exercises in various groups and settings. They provided me with invaluable feedback. I also wish to thank Elaine J. Ramshaw, professor of pastoral care at Methodist Theological School in Ohio, for the ideas and suggestions that came from her careful reading of the manuscript.

Chapter 1

How to Use Guided Imagery Exercises for Healing

The healing presence. We sense it when we read the Gospels. We affirm the healing Christ whom we find there. So full of healing are the Gospel accounts that it's hard to imagine what the story of Jesus would be like apart from his healing ministry. Jesus and "healing presence" belong together.

The promise of his healing presence is as real now as it was then. How can the promise be turned into reality? I know of no more effective tool for heightening our awareness of the healing presence of Christ than the active use of our imagination. The imagery exercises in this book will deepen your experience of his healing presence. Surely that is what Jesus intends, not just that we know about him and what he did for others but that we experience his healing presence in our lives today.

Though you may agree that it is possible to deepen your experience of Christ's healing presence through imaging, you may lack confidence in your ability to do so. This chapter contains all of the instruction you will need for your own personal use of these exercises or for serving as a guide to another person or group. After indicating more concretely what can be gained through the use of healing imagery as well as where and when it might be used, I will provide detailed instructions on the steps to follow for both personal and group use. If your use will be limited to personal meditation and prayer, you may wish to skip over the instructions provided for group use.

What Can Be Gained
Through the Use of These Exercises?

1. Making a Space. Guided imagery, as used in this volume, is a journey of the human spirit to a place filled with the loving and healing presence of God. Creating such a space is built into many of the exercises that follow, a place far removed from the stresses and strains of our harried lives, a place where we can experience peace and healing renewal. Is this just a form of escape? Not if your "inner space" is a centering point for wholeness and a secure place from which you can move decisively into the world.

2. Discerning the Need for Healing. Those who use these exercises are likely to be widely scattered on an illness–wellness continuum: some will be highly conscious of physical, mental, or spiritual problems; others will feel wonderfully well. Wherever you may be on such a continuum, there is value in discerning the need for healing and wellness. Guided imagery is a means for giving both illness and wellness a voice by listening to symptoms and signs and discerning their meaning.

3. Deepening the Awareness of the Healing Power of God. God can and does effect miraculous cures, but deepening awareness through imagery of the healing power of the gospel facilitates healing in much the same way as medication. It's not magic. It's not likely to be instantaneous. It's more like drawing on a spiritual resource of healing energy that effects physical as well as spiritual healing and well-being.

4. Giving New Life to the Healing Stories of Jesus. Though the healing stories of Jesus are still told and read with interest, we have become distanced from them through spiritualizing their meaning. Somewhat embarrassed by these accounts, the clergy generally feel more comfortable talking about spiritual rather than physical blindness or deafness, thus dismissing the actual accounts as quaint relics of a premedical era. In so doing, we deny ourselves access to the full healing power of these stories.

   It is my conviction that imagery can give new life to these stories by putting us in touch with the healing presence of

Christ. Can Christ really be present through imagery, or is that just a figment of the imagination? The psychological answer is that the image of Christ's healing presence is constructed with the aid of one's imagination. The theological answer is that Christ is really present in the deep structure of the imagery experience. The evidence for this is the effect of the experience in one's life: consolation, physical healing, a fresh infusion of joy and strength, and renewal of commitment.

5. Heightening the Expectant Trust of Faith. Perhaps the greatest value of guided imagery is that it stills the assertive ego by inducing a state of consciousness that is receptive to the healing presence of Christ. Feedback from church groups doing these exercises indicates very little conscious expectation of direct healing through prayer or any other church-related activity. However, these same people report a deepening of expectant trust in the healing presence of Christ while doing the exercises.

6. Promoting and Maintaining Wellness. Chapter 4 contains exercises that have wellness as their theme, such as "Transitions" and "Imaging the Image of God." The church is in a much better position than medicine to carry out a ministry of wellness, because it has direct and frequent access to the lives of people. Many churches are initiating wellness programs as part of their health and healing ministry, and imagery exercises will be a valuable resource for such ministry.

Where and When to Use
Guided Imagery for Healing and Wellness

1. Personal Meditation and Prayer. This is likely to be the most frequent way these exercises will be used. Though there are advantages to doing these exercises in the company of others, which will be noted in the pages to follow, there are also many advantages to individual use. You can choose the time and place for personal meditation and prayer, and that is its chief advantage. When you are aware of a need for healing, you can select the exercise that seems most appropriate to your particular need, find a location

that ensures privacy, and use your imagination to deepen the experience of Christ's healing presence.

2. Healing Services. A healing service is an ideal setting for an exercise in guided healing imagery. The liturgy is already a deeper-than-intellectual experience, making the transition to a level of consciousness appropriate for imagery easier than is the case in other settings. An imagery exercise can serve as a homily. Imagery can also be used in prayer or ministry to persons who come forward for anointing and laying on of hands.

3. Religious Retreat or Workshop. A retreat is an ideal setting for guided imagery, because those attending are not as likely to be bothered by distracting thoughts during times set aside for an inner journey. There will be a readiness, even a hunger for reflection on the need for healing and spiritual renewal. The same is true, though less so, for a workshop. A half-day workshop on health and healing is a good setting for introducing the practice of imagery to a group that is not familiar with it.

4. Bible Study or Adult Forum. Without knowing the term, many people are dispensationalists, believing that healing was true in the biblical era but not now. "Doing" the stories in the form of imagery can enable students of the Bible to revisit those times or put those stories into a modern context. As the leader becomes more familiar with the process of guided imagery, he or she can construct exercises based on other passages of the Bible related to healing.

5. Wellness Programs. Programs that promote good nutrition and healthy life-style would be enhanced by wellness exercises in guided imagery, as well as exercises in death education and grief work.

6. Youth Ministry. The movement from childhood through adolescence and young adulthood is arguably the most stress-filled time in the lives of most people. Learning exercises in relaxation and centering can help young people lay the foundation for a regular discipline of spiritual reflection throughout their lives.

7. Programs for Older Adults. Some of the exercises that follow are designed for older adults, and many others can be

easily adapted to meet the needs common to this age group. People at the later stages of life are often more reflective than they were at an earlier time, partly because they have more time for spiritual reflection and partly because so many of them have reached a stage of faith development that makes such reflection more natural. Most elderly people will also have more than one chronic illness to contend with, and drawing on inner spiritual resources through the use of imagery can help to promote a state of wellness even though chronic disorders remain.

Steps to Follow for Personal Use
Finding a Suitable Place

If meditation and personal prayer are not already built into your daily schedule, you will need to select a suitable place for doing these exercises. It should be a quiet place where you are not likely to be interrupted. Be sure to unplug the telephone and ask others not to disturb you. Choose a location where you feel comfortable, a place that invites meditation. In the winter a room with a fireplace is ideal.

Whatever the setting, it can be enhanced by such common Christian symbols as a lighted candle, an open Bible, or a cross. Choose a time of the day when you are experiencing low stress but are still able to remain mentally alert.

Choosing an Exercise and a Plan for Self-Guidance

Your choice of an exercise is crucial. It should be dictated by a diagnosis of your spiritual need and your sense that the exercise you've chosen will meet that need. Familiarity with all of the exercises through an initial reading will make that choice easier and more appropriate. Next, decide on a plan for guiding yourself through the exercise. If you are familiar with the exercise and have used it before, you will probably be able to read a portion of the exercise, such as a section between pauses, and then do the imaging that it calls for. However, if you're not familiar with the exercise, I would urge you to record the exercise first as if you were leading someone else; be sure to include the suggested pauses in your recording. Then you will be able to move more deeply into the exercise by listening to the recording and following its directions.

All imaging calls for guidance. Guiding yourself is less than ideal, since leading the exercise is a left-brain activity and doing the exercise is a right-brain activity. That's why following the direction of another person is the ideal, even if that other person is you on a tape recorder. Serving as your own guide while reading the exercise is more difficult, because it calls for frequent transitions between left-brain and right-brain activity. With practice you can do that quite smoothly, even when you are leading a group, but you will not likely achieve the depth of inner experience that comes when you are under the direction of a trusted guide.

Preparing Yourself

Preparation is always necessary when you are making a transition from one type of activity to another. You will know better than anyone else how to accomplish this. You need to be comfortable in order to fully relax. Wear loose clothing and take off your shoes. Allow yourself some time to relax before you begin the exercise. I find it helpful to play soft music and meditate on the presence of Christ in my life. This doesn't need to be more than five minutes, but providing some transition time between whatever you were doing before and the exercise you are about to begin will make it possible for you to move easily and smoothly into the exercise. Sitting erect in a comfortable chair with feet on the floor is better than lying down or relaxing in a recliner. The optimal body/mind state for effective imaging is being relaxed while remaining alert.

Doing the Exercise

Opening yourself to the healing presence of Christ is the key to an appropriate use of these exercises. Remember that Christ yearns for your healing and is reaching out to you with his healing presence. Your experience of his presence can come in many ways, not just through visual imagery. You may sense his presence as a beacon of light, a warm embrace, or a feeling of being loved and cared for. If you don't feel or sense God's healing presence during the exercise, it doesn't mean that you are not open to that presence.

Your faith is more than what you feel or sense at any particular time. God hears your prayer and surrounds you with healing love and power even when your feelings and intuitions do not discern God's healing presence.

One of the advantages of doing an exercise by yourself is that you can control the pace by stopping whenever you need more time to allow the experience to deepen or by moving forward at a quicker pace than suggested. Some people need longer periods of silence than others, and your own needs will vary from time to time. You don't always need to complete an exercise, and when your time is limited, you may decide to use only one portion of a particular exercise.

Most people feel freer to express their feelings in private than in groups. You may be moved to tears or experience inner pain when you uncover an emotional or spiritual wound that you had banned from conscious awareness. Express those feelings openly. That is part of the healing. At times you are likely to experience an inner resistance that blocks your full participation in a particular exercise or portion thereof. Don't fight that. The intention is to protect you from something that seems threatening. Simply offer that part of yourself to God for healing.

Many of the exercises have a writing portion. This is particularly valuable when these exercises are used privately. In fact, I would urge you to keep a journal to record your reflections, even when the exercise does not specifically call for writing. Such writing has a cumulative effect when it becomes part of a disciplined devotional practice. You will find yourself expressing things you did not know you felt or thought. Your journal can serve as a useful record of your spiritual struggles with forces of destruction and your experience of God's healing presence in the midst of those struggles.

Steps to Follow for Group Use

Finding a Suitable Place

I have done imagery exercises in busy, noisy places with hard chairs and elevated temperatures. If those doing the exercise are highly motivated and the leader does not make an issue out of adverse conditions, almost any place will work. However, distractions should be eliminated wherever possible. The biggest distraction for most people is noise, and noise from within the group, such as a beeper on a watch, is a bigger distraction than noise from outside the room, such as the sound of cars.

Examine the room that will be used with an eye and ear toward its use for guided imagery. Are the walls thin? Is there a radiator with a loud hiss or neon lights that buzz or flicker? Can the lights be dimmed or some of them turned off? If there is a telephone in the room, can it be unplugged?

Ideally the room should have good ventilation, mild to cool temperature, comfortable chairs, and a location where outside interruptions can be minimized.

Some common Christian symbol, such as a cross, a burning candle, or an open Bible, will help draw attention to the Christian context within which the imagery is done. Whatever symbol is used, it should be familiar to all those participating in the exercise, having the power to evoke a sense of mystery and deep meaning. The church sanctuary is an ideal place in terms of symbolic value, though there are likely to be some disadvantages as well, such as size, uncomfortable pews, and the possibility of interruptions.

Preparing the Participants

The more guided imagery I do, the more sensitive I become to the feelings of people who are uncomfortable with the process for whatever reason. It is never appropriate to impose a guided imagery exercise on a group. Explain the meaning of guided imagery and its proposed use to the group so that they know what to expect and are not misled by misconceptions. Let the group decide if they wish to proceed, and make sure that anyone who does not wish to participate can opt out without embarrassment. Securing agreement for using a guided imagery exercise as a homily in a healing service may not be feasible, but at the very least an announcement should be made well in advance of the service.

Those who feel unsure about doing guided imagery for the first time may find some reassurance from the experience of people who participated in the testing of the exercises in this volume. Among 417 participants in church groups of various sizes, 185 reported that this was their first experience with guided imagery. Only 24 of the 417 indicated that they had no interest in doing guided imagery again.

For groups that have not used imagery before, the purpose of inducing relaxation and using background music should be explained. Participants should be assured that they will at all times remain in complete control of the experience and that they can withdraw from the experience anytime they wish by simply ignoring the directions being given or by substituting something more appropriate for themselves, which people do regularly. Having given them these assurances, the leader should encourage those doing the exercise to enter as fully as they can into the experience by trusting the spiritual direction they are being given.

It will be helpful for those doing the exercise to know in advance that there will be brief periods of silence for reflecting on some aspect of their inner journey. It might be wise to comment on the value of silence, noting why most Americans are uncomfortable with it.

If a particular exercise has a writing portion to it, explain the purpose it serves. Make sure that every person is equipped with paper and pen. Assure those doing the exercise that whatever they write is between themselves and God.

Inducing a State of Relaxation and Readiness

Guided imagery calls for a level of awareness deeper than the ordinary, everyday consciousness of the waking day. A state of relaxation somewhere between waking and sleeping facilitates the journey inward, where images are a much more natural and spontaneous form of expression than concepts or abstract ideas.

Keep the relaxation factor in mind when choosing the location for doing imagery. Comfortable chairs should be provided whenever possible. If the room is large enough and the floor is carpeted, you may want to suggest the option of lying down. This will enhance the relaxation (sometimes too much), but it creates a problem if writing is part of the exercise. Lights that can be dimmed will also help.

I generally play a tape recording of soft background music to facilitate relaxation. Most people find this helpful. Not any music will do. Music with words, a strong melody, or a pronounced beat will draw attention to itself and away from inner reflection. Some people, particularly musicians, will be distracted no matter what music you choose. I recommend the music of Steven Halpern, such as *Comfort Zone* or *Soft Focus.*

Each of the exercises in this volume has an opening section designed to induce relaxation and a state of readiness for guided imagery, some tailored specifically for a particular exercise, others interchangeable. The leader may take elements from a number of exercises to construct his or her own induction exercise.

Those doing the exercise will regularly be asked to focus their attention on their breathing in the relaxation portion of the exercises. Being attuned to the natural rhythm of the human body helps center the self. Breathing comes from the roots of our being and has profound religious meaning to Christians. Life comes into Adam's body through the breath of God (Gen. 2:7), and the Holy Spirit comes to the disciples through the breath of Jesus (John 20:22).

Leading the Guided Imagery

The effect of imagery is determined to a large degree by pacing and tone of voice. Proper pacing calls for frequent pauses and slower speech than normal. I have suggested appropriate places for pauses, most of which occur in the induction. Three dots . . . represent a short pause (about 3 seconds); five dots . . . . . represent a longer pause (about 6 seconds). Pauses are also needed in the guided imagery portion, and a suggested length is given for longer pauses. The appropriate length of any pause is a matter of judgment, dependent on a number of variables, such as time and place.

Don't judge the length of pauses on the basis of your own perception of the passing of time. The pause will seem longer to you than to those you are guiding, because time always seems to go more slowly for those who are keeping track of it. Get feedback about pacing from those doing the exercise. Chances are that you'll need to slow down rather than speed up, at least initially. The length of pauses will also be determined by the nature of the group and the setting for the exercises. For example, longer pauses would be more appropriate in a retreat setting than in a Sunday morning Bible class. Experience will be your best teacher.

Your tone of voice is also crucial for leading these exercises. A soft, gentle voice is best. If the group is large — and these exercises work well in a large group — it is better to amplify the voice than to make it strident. Rather than drawing attention to you, your voice should sound as if it comes from inside the persons you are directing. Listening to yourself on a tape recorder and getting feedback from those doing the exercise will help you make whatever adjustments are necessary to develop an effective tonal quality.

Though pacing and tone of voice are important, the content of the exercise determines its worth. The leader should not only be familiar but comfortable with the content of these exercises. If an exercise does not ring true for you, your discomfort will be conveyed through your tone of voice. Change what seems inappropriate. Add what you think is missing. Eliminate what seems superfluous or distracting. In other words, make the exercise your own. After you become more familiar with the process, you should be able to construct an exercise of your own, based either on one of your favorite portions of Scripture or on some particular need, such as a person with a particular kind of illness or emotional problem.

The Writing Portion of the Exercise

The writing portion included in many of the exercises can be their greatest value for some people, but people who rarely do much writing may feel awkward when asked to do so. Some settings make writing problematic. For example, it is difficult to write without tables or desk chairs. Though I consider writing to be a central component of many of the exercises, it can be eliminated with only minor adaptations.

Encourage spontaneous writing rather than exposition or interpretation. The best writing will not be about the imagery but an expression of it. Interpretation calls for analysis and critique, useful tools for evaluation, but guaranteed to short-circuit the process of guided imagery.

Unless those doing the exercise are naturally intuitive or have kept a personal journal of some kind, they are not likely to have done much writing that could be called a spontaneous expression of inner experience. Those for whom writing is a chore or always logic-centered will often report that the deeply relaxed and intuitive level of experience was lost when they were asked to write. You will need to encourage those doing the exercise to let their pens simply be a medium for expressing what they are experiencing.

The writing does not have to be in the form of sentences. It might be a series or cluster of words or phrases. In fact, it is better if the writing is not linear, the very form of which (line by line) implies a left-brain, logic-centered mode of thinking. Suggest the idea of putting separate words in a cluster, letting feelings and ideas flow out of that center. You may want to ask those doing the exercise to draw rather than write. Be sure to provide appropriate materials (crayons and chalk).

One way to retain a deeper level of experience while writing is to open the eyes only partially while writing and then close them again to avoid distraction. Putting the pen down on the table when not writing is also a subtle reminder to keep the attention focused inward. Above all, the writing needs to be understood as an expression of experience, not a description of it and certainly not an analysis or critique of it.

Writing integrates the imagery experience and makes it available for reflection at a later time. Encourage those doing the exercise to read their accounts out loud, either after the group has done the exercise or in private. Reading in a group is not done for purposes of sharing with others but to deepen the inner experience. A further dimension of feedback comes through reading entries made one, two, or ten years before. If individuals or groups use these exercises regularly, they should be encouraged to date their accounts and keep them in a journal.

Closing the Exercise

After allowing sufficient time for writing or reflection, the task of the leader is to gently lead those doing the exercise out of the guided imagery experience and back into the world of everyday experience. I have suggested the amount of time to be allowed for writing and/or reflection at the end of each of the exercises, but the leader will need to use his or her judgment about whether to allow more or less time than that. During a retreat or a workshop, adults can be expected to use as much time for writing as you will allow. Five minutes is a sufficient though minimal amount of time for almost any exercise. It is better to eliminate the writing portion if less time than that is available.

The transition from a deep inner experience to an ordinary level of consciousness should be gradual and gentle. After you have directed the persons doing the exercise to return from the inner world of their experience to the place you are located, allow sufficient time to complete the transition process. Since the leader does not have to make this transition, it is easy to underestimate the time that is needed. Continue to play the background music during the transition period; shutting it off will break the mood and signal the end of the exercise.

Group Discussion and Feedback

Should there be discussion at the end of the exercise? If so, what kind? These are questions of judgment, based on the type of group and the time available. There is only one cardinal rule: No one should be pressed into sharing his or her experience. As a general rule, groups do benefit from the opportunity to share their thoughts about the experience. The purpose of the discussion is not therapy but integration of the experience.

It is important to get feedback on your performance as a leader, but that's not likely to happen in a group discussion, especially if the comments are negative. Instead, ask those doing the exercise to respond in writing to questions such as the following: What did you find most striking and most disconcerting during the exercise? How would you rate the leader in terms of tone of voice, pace, length of pauses, and length of exercise? The chief value of the responses you will get, if my experience is any indicator, is not the feedback on your performance but the many expressions of what a powerful tool imagery can be.

Factors Working
Against Effective Use of Imagery

Logic-centered individuals who want structure in their lives are more likely to experience resistance to the process than those who give free rein to their imagination. Men are more likely to fit this category than women. Men are culturally conditioned to be rational and logical in their thinking, "macho" in their behavior, and detached from their feelings. These are broad generalizations, of course, and changes are taking place, but it is my experience that men find less value and meaning in guided imagery than women.

Restlessness of body, mind, and spirit works against effective use of imagery. For the active person, guided imagery is a complete switch of gears: from busyness to inactivity, from noisiness to quiet, from outside involvement to inner reflection. That change of pace is difficult even for those who have experience in doing imagery. The cardinal rule is not to fight restlessness, which only increases it, but to ignore it and the intruding thoughts that it elicits. Most of the time the restlessness will subside as the relaxation deepens, but sometimes the guided imagery will simply not work.

There will be occasions for every individual when guided imagery will not work. The reasons are legion: lack of energy, physical or mental weariness, spiritual dryness, restlessness, low-grade depression, pain from some physical malady, the content of a particular exercise. Those doing the exercise should be reminded that since this has happened to even the most celebrated mystics, they can assume it will happen to them also.

Some people will find themselves fighting sleep or actually dozing off during the exercise. This is to be expected, especially if the exercise comes at the end of a busy day or after a meal. For the exercise to succeed it is necessary to induce a state of relaxation that is close to sleeping. To defuse feelings of failure for those who do drift into sleep, tell people in advance that if they fall asleep they probably need that more than the exercise. When possible, encourage those doing the exercise to take a fifteen-minute nap before attending a session where guided imagery will be used.

Improving Your Skill as a Leader

Participation in guided imagery is both a necessary and sufficient condition for serving as a leader in such exercises. It is a necessary condition because you cannot have a feel for and appreciation of guided imagery unless you have done it yourself. It is a sufficient condition because no other training or experience is needed to be an effective leader.

If you can't be a participant in a group led by another, read one of the exercises into a tape recorder as if you were guiding another person through the exercise. Then be guided through the exercise by listening to yourself on the tape. This means submitting yourself to the full discipline of the exercise, including the writing portion.

It is also valuable to listen to yourself as a leader in order to evaluate your performance. Listen to the tone of your voice. Is it gentle or harsh? Soft or hard? Soothing or abrasive? Listen to the pace. Is it fast or slow? Jerky or smooth? Listen to the emotional quality of your voice. Is it warm and inviting or cool and aloof? Flat or full of feeling? Leading one person through an exercise and getting direct feedback is also helpful for evaluating your performance. Finally, ask for feedback in writing from the first groups you lead, making sure that the responses are anonymous.

Conclusion

Guided imagery is a powerful tool for activating the imagination in any area of faith and life, and the imaging of faith in relation to healing and wellness is no exception. This is the case whether or not those doing the exercise are in need of healing for some particular malady. The greatest benefit that can come from using these exercises is a heightened awareness of the healing presence of Christ. Awakening faith in Christ the Healer is the first step in any program of health education within the church, and these exercises will be useful for that purpose.

You have been given a rationale for guided imagery and a step-by-step procedure for using it. In the last analysis, however, you will need to try these exercises before you can make a judgment about their usefulness. After you've read through the exercises, choose one that seems most appealing to you and try it out on yourself or a relatively small group of people, assembled perhaps for the purpose of helping you to evaluate this resource for ministry. Not until you've done at least one such experiment are you ready to make a judgment about the usefulness of imagery for healing.

Chapter 2

Exercises Based on the Healing Stories of Jesus

Each exercise in this chapter uses one of the healing stories in the Gospels as its point of departure. These narratives are the master stories of healing for Christians in every age and every culture. However varied the interpretation of these stories in different historical and cultural settings, they have provided both inspiration and guidance for the Christian ministry of healing down through the centuries. As the core of the church's tradition of healing, these stories are frequently used as Scripture readings and sermon texts in worship services. We deepen our identity as the healing church in this way and renew our commitment to carry out the mission of healing that Jesus so clearly mandates by his example and command.

In some instances more than one exercise is based on the same healing story. Sometimes the exercise draws people into the original story, similar to a "you were there" TV documentary. At other times the exercise reframes the story as a contemporary event. In either case those doing the exercise are drawn into the story as recipients of healing or spiritual guidance. When portions of the healing stories are included in an exercise, the New Revised Standard Version (NRSV) is used.

The introduction to each exercise provides some background information to the particular healing story being used as well as some helpful hints concerning the use of the exercise.

Healing of the Paralytic

MARK 2:1–12

Introduction

The healing of the paralytic is one of the best-known healing stories in the Gospels. There is high drama throughout the narrative: the sick man on a stretcher being dropped through the roof of a house, a heated controversy between Jesus and the scribes, and a paralyzed man picking up his stretcher and walking through a crowded room of dumbfounded people.

The story has a number of striking characteristics. As in other stories, faith is a factor in healing — not the faith of the paralytic but of the four who bring him to Jesus. What about the paralytic? Was it also his faith that Jesus saw? We don't know that for sure, but we can assume that he would not have agreed to come without some degree of expectant trust in the healing power of Jesus.

Another striking characteristic of this story is the ease with which Jesus moves back and forth between healing and forgiveness. When you expect Jesus to heal this man who has obviously been brought to him for that purpose, he forgives him. When you expect Jesus to forgive as a demonstration of his authority, he heals. This jars us because we think that healing is directed to a physical need and forgiveness to a spiritual need. Our categories are too narrow to grasp what is happening. Bodily healing and forgiveness are two aspects of a larger whole, and it is this larger whole or the whole person that Jesus is concerned with in his ministry — both then and now.

A third noteworthy characteristic of this story is the scribes' lack of faith. They come to Jesus with an attitude that makes it very difficult for them to see the unfolding of God's mercy and love right in front of their eyes. Rather than dismissing them too quickly as closed-minded clods, we might do better to examine our own lack of faith in the healing presence of Christ within the church today.

There are two separate exercises based on this story. The first is a reenactment of the story in a modern setting. The second uses the story as a background for focusing on the problem of paralysis — physical, emotional, or spiritual. Both exercises depend on the willingness of the person doing the exercise to identify with the paralytic by focusing on some form of physical or spiritual paralysis.

EXERCISE 1, HEALING OF THE PARALYTIC

Guided Imagery

Be as relaxed as you can where you are sitting . . . releasing all the tension within your body . . . feeling the tension melt away like snow under the rays of a warm sun . . . letting your eyes close or keeping them focused on one particular spot to keep yourself from being distracted by what is going on outside you . . . concentrating your attention on inner awareness . . . breathing naturally and slowly . . . inhaling deeply the life-giving oxygen of the air around you and exhaling all tensions and poisons from your body . . . breathing in . . . and breathing out . . . breathing in . . . and breathing out . . . feeling the relaxation deepen . . . letting your awareness shift from what is happening outside you to what is happening within you . . . letting yourself feel a oneness with your body and a deep sense of wonder at the mystery of its simple and yet infinitely complex operation. (*Pause for 30 seconds*)

In your mind's eye picture yourself in bed in a room where you have been for the last ten years of your life. It might be your bedroom or any other room that would be appropriate if you were bedfast with a long-term chronic illness. Furnish the room any way that you wish . . . . . Let yourself feel the frustration of being trapped in that room . . . in that bed . . . day after day . . . month after month . . . year after year . . . completely dependent on others to take care of you and completely helpless to do anything to improve your condition. Look at the ceiling and the four walls and imagine never being able to see beyond the walls

of a room that has become your prison. (*Pause for 30 seconds*)
From within the body of a person who is paralyzed, imagine holding a little bird gently but securely in your hands. Imagine that the little bird is you, trapped in your body and yearning to be free, feeling helpless to effect any change in your situation. (*Pause for 30 seconds*)

In your mind's eye picture someone you know coming into your room with news that Jesus has just arrived in the town where you live and will be visiting the church you attend. The person who comes into the room can be anybody you choose, a friend or member of your family . . . He or she wants to find three others to help transport you to the church and hurries off before you have a chance to respond. As you lie in bed, reflecting on your illness and the prospect of being taken to Jesus, what are your feelings? You've lived with this paralysis so long, invested so much energy in learning to accept the limits imposed by your condition. Dare you hope that it might be different? What will people think when they parade you in there? What if nothing happens? What then? And what if you are freed from your paralysis? What then? What will people expect of you? What will you expect of yourself? (*Pause for 1 minute*)

Your friend or family member returns with three other friends of yours. They can be anybody you choose, each with sufficient strength to carry you. Take a moment to decide who they will be. (*Pause for 20 seconds*) Picture yourself being transported by them to the church. Notice the staring eyes of people when they notice your condition, eyes that are quickly diverted when your glance meets theirs. Does this exposure of your paralysis and dependency make you wish that you could return to the security of the isolation you have grown accustomed to? (*Pause for 30 seconds*)

Imagine yourself arriving at the church where Jesus is speaking and discovering that a huge crowd has filled the church to overflowing. Your friends try unsuccessfully to persuade people to let them through. What are you thinking and feeling as this goes on? Are you angry? . . . embarrassed? . . . feeling helpless? . . . maybe enjoying the attention? (*Pause for 30 seconds*)

In your mind's eye imagine some ingenious method that your friends use to get you to Jesus, perhaps lowering you from the balcony or using some other scheme that comes into your mind—the more bizarre the better. (*Pause for 30 seconds*) What is going on inside you as they execute this plan, so intent on their task that they seem oblivious of you? Are you offering them encouragement or protesting the absurdity of their behavior? Their plan succeeds and soon your stretcher lies at the feet of Jesus, who looks first at your friends and then directly at you. What do you see in his eyes and in the expression on his face? What do you expect from him? Reproach for being so ill-mannered and so demanding of attention? Encouragement to be strong and of good faith? Your neediness is very great. Would you dare to ask for what you need? (*Pause for 30 seconds*)

Jesus looks intently at you and says, "My child, your sins are forgiven." How do you respond to those words? Are you surprised? Is Jesus suggesting that you are responsible for your paralysis? Might there be some way you have contributed to your paralysis? Take a moment to reflect on these words of forgiveness that are so unexpected. (*Pause for 1 minute*)

As you struggle to understand the meaning of Jesus' words, be aware of an argument going on between him and some people who have criticized him for forgiving your sins since only God can do that. What are you feeling as that argument grows more and more heated? Are you angry at those people for being so oblivious of you and your condition? Are you angry at Jesus for being drawn into that argument and thinking of you only as an object lesson? Or are you feeling that you and your problem aren't really that important? (*Pause for 30 seconds*)

Now picture Jesus concluding the argument by telling them he will demonstrate that he has power to forgive sins. He turns to you and says: "Stand up, take your mat and go to your home." From within the experience of being paralyzed in body or in spirit, imagine Jesus saying those words to you. Let the experience deepen until you are sure of your response to Jesus deep within the center of yourself. And then without feeling rushed, let the story conclude in any way that seems appropriate to you. (*Pause for 2 minutes*)

As you are ready, return to this room and reorient yourself to this place, refreshed and renewed by your encounter with the healing presence and power of Jesus.

EXERCISE 2, HEALING THE PARALYTIC IN YOU

Guided Imagery

Be as relaxed as you can where you are sitting . . . releasing all the tension within your body . . . feeling the tension melt away like snow under the rays of a warm sun . . . letting your eyes close or keeping them focused on one particular spot to keep yourself from being distracted by what is going on outside you . . . concentrating your attention on inner awareness . . . breathing naturally and slowly . . . inhaling deeply the life-giving oxygen of the air around you and exhaling all tensions and poisons from your body . . . breathing in . . . and breathing out . . . breathing in . . . and breathing out . . . feeling the relaxation deepen . . . letting your awareness shift from what is happening outside you to what is happening within you . . . letting yourself feel a oneness with your body and a deep sense of wonder at the mystery of its simple and yet infinitely complex operation. (*Pause for 30 seconds*)

In your mind's eye imagine yourself either partially or completely paralyzed. You can decide how complete the paralysis is, but it should be severe enough to keep you bedfast and dependent on others for your care. Imagine what you would look like and how you would feel after a prolonged period of being confined to bed and dependent on others for your care. I will give you a moment to enter deeply and fully into that scene until you are that paralyzed person and view this scene from within that paralyzed body. (*Pause for 2 minutes*)

From within this experience of yourself as paralyzed, ask yourself the question, "Who is the paralytic within me? What within me resonates most fully with the feeling of being paralyzed?" Are there parts of your body that are stiff, no longer functioning smoothly? Is there something in your behavior that is paralyzed, making it difficult for you to assert yourself or reach out to someone whose support you need? Or maybe you are aware of a rigidity in your behavior that makes you resistant to change. I'll give you a moment to get in touch with the paralytic in you. (*Pause for 1 minute*)

Imagine that Jesus was born in this century rather than the first century. He has a reputation as a modern-day healer, and you have just heard that he is coming to the town where you live. How would you react to the news of his coming? How do you feel about healers and the claims made by them? Are you the kind of person who would go to a healer? If Jesus were your contemporary, how would he be the same, and how different, from modern-day healers? Take a moment to reflect on the healing presence of Jesus and what he might do for the paralytic in you. (*Pause for 1 minute*) If you think that Jesus can be of some help to you, however you conceive of that, imagine how you can get to him, enlisting whatever support you need to accomplish that. I'll give you a moment to let that unfold in your mind. (*Pause for 1 minute*)

Imagine yourself in the presence of Jesus, surrounded by many people who are eager to see and hear him. It can be a place of your choosing, indoors or outdoors, anyplace that seems appropriate to you. Do you feel like you have a right to be there? What are your expectations? Are you hopeful or skeptical, or maybe both at the same time? Look at the face of Jesus as he turns to you. What is the expression on his face as he looks at you, and how does that make you feel? What do you want to ask him? (*Pause for 30 seconds*)

Before you can ask or say anything, Jesus says to you: "My child, your sins are forgiven." Is that what you were going to request from him? What do you suppose prompted him to say that? Is he suggesting that you are responsible for your paralysis? How might that be? Is it possible that at some level you really chose to be this way, that you have contributed to your condition of powerlessness? Or is he trying to tell you that your sins are your chief problem, not your paralysis? "My child, your sins are forgiven. My child, your sins are forgiven." Let the words echo through your mind as you repeat them to yourself, "My child, your sins are forgiven." (*Pause for 30 seconds*)

Suddenly you are aware of a controversy that has broken out between Jesus and the church leaders who are there. They are critical of him for forgiving sins when he's not even ordained, much less divine. How are you feeling as that battle wages? Give yourself a voice to respond to what is happening. Let the voice be an expression of your need and your faith. (*Pause for 30 seconds*)

Jesus concludes the argument by telling his critics that he will demonstrate that he has power to forgive sins. Imagine that Jesus turns to you and speaks directly to the paralysis in you, telling you what you need to know and do about that paralysis. Then respond to what Jesus tells you in a manner that feels right to you. Let that scene unfold naturally and then bring it to a close in any way that seems appropriate to you. (*Pause for 1–2 minutes*)

As you are ready, open your eyes and reorient yourself to this room and its surroundings, with a feeling of freedom and spontaneity in body, mind, and spirit.

Healing of the Leper

LUKE 5:12–15

Introduction

Leprosy has always had a stigma attached to it, and those who have contracted the disease have almost universally been ostracized by society. That makes a story about leprosy a good point of departure for dealing with contemporary illnesses that have a stigma attached to them, such as AIDS and cancer. It makes it a story that is difficult to identify with, though, because not only is the disease repulsive and alienating, it is also foreign to the experience of most Westerners.

For the Jews leprosy was a symbol of the effect of sin in a person's life. Both sin and leprosy brought a separation from God and others. Both sin and leprosy work silently and secretly to disfigure, desensitize, and defile. Small wonder, then, that the term *cleanse* rather than *heal* was most frequently used to describe the cure of leprosy. The problem with such a close connection between sin and leprosy is that it can suggest that leprosy is caused by sin and that the leper is being punished by God. Though there is a relationship between sin and illness, we are in no position to pass judgment on the sick. Jesus refused to condemn the ill, even when invited to do so (John 9:1–5); instead he used the occasion to show the mercy of God.

One of the most striking characteristics of this healing story is that Jesus touches the leper as he heals him, an act that must have had a powerful effect on a person regarded by everybody, including the leper, as untouchable. The use of touch is optional in this exercise at the point in the story where Jesus touches the leper. Touch was included when this exercise was tested; most participants found it meaningful, but others were distracted by it. Clear instructions about this should be given at the beginning of the exercise, such as who touches whom and for how long. One of those doing the exercise suggested that it would be less distracting if the leader were able to touch each of the participants. I would recommend that practice if there are no more than ten in the group.

The story from Luke should be read before the exercise begins, preferably from the NRSV. Writing can be substituted for the portion of the exercise devoted to imaginary sharing with a friend, as well as actual sharing time after the exercise is completed.

Guided Imagery

Relieve the tension in your body by stretching the muscles in your arms and legs and then relaxing them. (*Pause for 10 seconds*) Next rotate your neck on its axis, first one way and then the other. (*Pause for 10 seconds*) Finally, move your shoulders up and around. (*Pause for 10 seconds. The leader should demonstrate each of these actions while giving the instruction*) Take several deep breaths, letting yourself go limp as you exhale. (*Pause for 30 seconds*) Pay attention to your breathing. Notice how easily each breath comes and goes, without effort or strain on your part. As you turn your attention inward, let your eyes close or keep them focused on one place so that you can avoid being distracted by what is going on outside you . . . letting your breathing come evenly and slowly . . . moving the center of your attention more and more to the inner world of your experience . . . letting all worries or distracting thoughts simply float by until they are no longer within the realm of your consciousness . . . feeling the goodness of moving to a safe haven within yourself while maintaining a close connection with others who are engaging in the same kind of experience as you.

With the aid of your imagination, create a room deep inside yourself and furnish it in any way you like—perhaps with a recliner that faces a large picture window overlooking a lake, a mountain, or whatever scenery deepens your sense of the presence of God. The room you have created is for you and you alone, and yet you remain connected to every other person around you who shares your experience of solitude and connectedness. (*Pause for 20 seconds*)

Imagine what it would have been like to have been the person described by Luke as "full of leprosy." The disease far advanced, you have sores covering your entire body. Portions of your body, such as your hands, are without any sensation of touch; the leprosy has destroyed the nerve endings. Feeling no hot or cold or pressure, you are subject to serious injury without even being aware of it. As a good Jew you would know the Levitical command: "The leper . . . shall wear torn clothes and let the hair of his head hang loose and he shall cover his upper lip and cry, 'Unclean, Unclean.'" Imagine yourself in such a condition: sores over your whole body, torn clothes, long, disheveled hair, forced to pronounce yourself unclean when anybody is within sight. I'll give you a moment to deepen the experience of physical suffering and social isolation that was the inevitable lot of every leper. (*Pause for 30 seconds*)

Turn your attention now to the leprosy you presently experience within yourself or fear in the future. It may be the leprosy of cancer, not only the disease but the social stigma that goes with it. It may be the leprosy of AIDS or the fear of having the HIV virus, not only the disease but the social stigma that goes with it. It may be the leprosy of alcoholism, not only the disease but the social stigma of being an alcoholic. It may be the leprosy of some secret sin that grows within you despite repeated efforts to root it out. Reflect for a moment on the leprosy within you, whatever it is that isolates you from others, that makes you feel unclean and uncared-for. To deepen the experience of isolation, imagine yourself telling everyone you meet every day about the leprosy within yourself, and then picture the look on their faces as they draw back in horror. (*Pause for 1 minute*)

Imagine that you have heard that Jesus is nearby. You want to seek him out and ask him to heal the leprosy within you, but you know that you are an outcast, destined to live in isolation. Knowing that you are considered unclean and unworthy, would you have the courage to break through those barriers and approach him? Imagine yourself standing before Jesus, telling him openly about the leprosy within you, and saying, "Lord, if you choose, you can make me clean." (*Pause for 45 seconds*)

As you kneel before Jesus with head bowed, imagine the touch of his hand on your head or shoulders, followed by the words: "I do choose. Be made clean." (*Optional instruction: Reach out your hand and gently touch the person next to you.*) Experience the healing power of a touch that reaches across the barriers that have isolated you from others and left you alone and uncared for. Let the assurance of Jesus' unconditional love penetrate deeply into the center of your self, filling your spirit with a sense of Jesus' healing presence. Imagine the healing power of Jesus' touch penetrating to the heart of the leprosy within you and loosening its grip on you. Imagine yourself as Jesus intends you to be, whole in body, mind, and spirit. (*Pause for 1 minute*)

In your imagination, tell the story of what happened to you to someone else. It can be anyone you choose. What would you say about what happened to you, about the difference between before and after your encounter with Jesus? Be perfectly honest. If nothing happened, acknowledge that. If something surprising occurred, express that. Then talk with this person about how you are different as a result of the experience and how that will affect the rest of your life. After you've told your story, listen carefully to how this person responds to what you've said. I'll give you time to let that unfold. (*Pause for 2 minutes*)

As you are ready, let the experience draw to a close, open your eyes, and reorient yourself to this room, feeling refreshed and renewed in body, mind, and spirit.

The Good Samaritan

LUKE 10:25–37

Introduction

There is no finer model for caring than the one provided by this gentle Samaritan, and we do well to use him as an example. But for everyone who cares there must be someone who is cared for. We generally get very little help and encouragement in learning to be cared for. When was the last time you heard a sermon in which you were asked to identify with the man who lies beaten and abandoned by the side of the road? Can we recognize ourselves in this person and admit that we can be as needy as he, not only in relation to God but in relation to each other?

It is not likely that many of us will find ourselves in as desperate and helpless a position as he, and that's part of the problem. Most of our wounds are well hidden. We've been taught to cover them up with a smiling face and a stiff upper lip. We've also been taught to identify with the strong, the successful, the winners. We've been taught that tears are a sign of weakness, to be shed, if at all, in private. We've been taught to solve our own problems and not to burden others with them, especially people who are busy and have more important things to do.

This guided imagery exercise is done from the perspective of the wounded and helpless man. Its goal is to help us realize that we are all beggars before God, all totally dependent on the gifts that God so freely bestows, including the gift of healing. The exercise is a lesson in graciously receiving the gifts of healing that come to us from God through others, and especially when we are totally dependent on the care of others. In one sense that's true all the time, but we still hold tightly to the myth of our independence and self-sufficiency. This exercise offers the person doing it an opportunity to experience the vulnerability of being helpless and totally dependent on the care of others.

Jesus is normally identified with the good Samaritan, the one who does the caring and serves as the model for our caring. However, in the parable of the last judgment (Matthew 25), Jesus is identified with the one who is cared for: the person in prison, the person who is hungry and without clothes, the person in need. It's obvious to us that Christ is in the caring, that he works in and through us when we care for others. It's not as obvious that Jesus is on the receiving end of care, that he is in our suffering and in the receiving of care that others provide for us. It is no disgrace to be helpless and abandoned and totally dependent on the care and healing of others; at no time is our Lord nearer to us than then.

The persons doing this exercise should be prepared for what is to come. If you are leading the exercise, I would suggest reading the parable of the good Samaritan or briefly retelling it. Participants should be told that they will be asked to identify with the helpless person in the parable and not with the Samaritan. The purpose is to help them face such experiences with faith and to learn how to receive care graciously. This exercise is fairly long and may need to be abridged for some purposes.

Guided Imagery

Relax as fully as you can in the chair where you are sitting, preferably with your feet flat on the floor and your back straight. Be sensitive to the natural rhythm of your breathing . . . breathing in . . . and breathing out . . . letting your breathing be natural, with no effort other than that supplied by the spontaneous movement of your diaphragm . . . breathing evenly and slowly . . . becoming more and more relaxed . . . drifting slowly down, deeper and deeper toward the center of your inner self . . . becoming more and more relaxed and at the same time more and more sensitive to the inner world of your experience . . . turning your vision inward in order to be in closer touch with what you would never expose to others and sometimes not even yourself . . . letting all distractions fade into the background of your consciousness . . . drifting deeper and deeper into the inner world of your experience . . . distancing yourself from any sounds that you hear in this room or outside this room until they seem far away and unimportant . . . concentrating your attention only on the inner world of your awareness. (*Pause for 30 seconds*)

From within the world of your inner experience, imagine a series of events in your life that leave you in a helpless and desperate physical state. It need not be anything you fear in the discernible future, but it should be something you can realistically imagine and perhaps already have. Do that now. Imagine yourself as so physically helpless that you are totally dependent on the care of others. The condition may be the result of an illness or an accident. A number of possibilities are likely to come to mind, perhaps from a memory of helplessness out of your own past or your close contact with someone else who has been in such a condition. Briefly consider each possibility and then choose the one that most vividly and realistically gives you the feeling of being helpless and out of control. I'll give you time for that story to unfold and for the experience to deepen. (*Pause for 1 minute*)

Picture your surroundings. It can be anywhere that fits with the condition of helplessness you are imagining. It may be that you are lying battered and abandoned somewhere by the side of the road, like the man in Jesus' parable. Or you may be in a hospital bed somewhere or perhaps at home in a state of deep depression because of some personal tragedy. Trust your intuition about where you find yourself and how you are feeling. Pay close attention to your physical and emotional condition. (*Pause for 30 seconds*)

How well are you able to cope with feelings of helplessness? What seems important to you? Evaluate your priorities in life. How are they different from when you felt well and in full control of what was happening to you? How strong is your faith? Do you feel that God has deserted you or that you are being punished? Are you asking, Why me? Or do you feel closer to God because of your condition? What are your physical needs? . . . Your emotional needs? . . . Your spiritual needs? (*Pause for 1 minute*)

From within the experience of helplessness, express yourself in prayer to Jesus. Let the prayer be a free-flowing expression of your feelings and needs, with no attempt on your part to censor or alter the stream of consciousness that comes forth. As the words begin to come, write them down as if you were speaking directly to Jesus. (*Allow 3 minutes for writing*)

In your mind's eye picture Jesus coming to you, wherever you imagine yourself to be. He has heard your prayer and come in response to it. Imagine Jesus placing his hands on your head or shoulders or wherever the pain is—healing hands, gentle hands. He knows without your telling him where you need to be touched. Feel a healing power like a surge of energy flow from his hands through your entire body. Like a warm current, the healing energy radiates from his hands and permeates your entire body, easing any tension that is there and stimulating the healing forces within your body. Imagine the gentle, healing hands of Jesus touching you wherever you feel the need for this warm and caring expression of his love for you and his desire that you be made whole. (*Pause for 1 minute*)

Imagine other ways that Jesus attends to your pain and suffering. It can be anything your imagination suggests, anything from talking with you, to binding up your wounds like the good Samaritan, to tending a wounded body part, to preparing you for death. Be honest with yourself about the expectations of your faith. Don't indulge in a fantasy that doesn't fit with your image of Jesus and his relationship to you. Take time to reflect on the healing presence of Jesus in your life in any way that seems appropriate to you. (*Pause for 1–2 minutes*)

What provisions does Jesus make for you as he prepares to leave? What does he say to your physician, your nurse, your priest or pastor, and anyone else providing therapy for you? Above all, what does he say to you about your feelings of helplessness? About your faith? About the meaning of life? About your hope for the future? As you are ready, begin a dialogue with Jesus about what you have been experiencing. Write "J" at the beginning of the line where Jesus is speaking and your initial at the beginning of the line where you are speaking. Let the dialogue flow freely, trusting your sense of what Jesus would say to you and you to Jesus. (*Allow 10–15 minutes for writing*)

Bring this time with Jesus to a close in any way that seems appropriate. Perhaps it may be saying good-bye, with assurances that Jesus will always return in time of need. Or you may imagine Jesus taking you with him. Do whatever seems appropriate. When that is concluded, return to this room with renewed trust that nothing can separate you from the love of God in Christ Jesus. (*Pause for 1–2 minutes*)

Healing at the Pool of Bethesda

JOHN 5:1–18

Introduction

The association of healing with a body of water or a spring appears frequently in every age and every culture. Water is a powerful symbol of purification, healing, power, and life. The waters of baptism are an expression of life-giving power for Christians.

The question Jesus asks in the story seems ironic: "Do you want to be made well?" The man had been there for thirty-eight years trying to keep the hope alive that he might be the first one to get to the pool! Jesus knows that, as John indicates in the narrative, and still he asks. Jesus appears to be testing the motivation and determination of the man to be healed, and perhaps also checking the resistance to being healed. Had he become so identified with his illness that he had no identity apart from it?

There can be no healing until the sick person wants to be healed. The unequivocal desire for recovery is an important ingredient in the "expectant trust" that Jerome Frank has identified as the means by which a person participates in his or her healing. One way to test your desire for recovery from illness is to list on one side of a piece of paper all of the reasons you want to be well and then alongside it all of the reasons for keeping things as they are, such as not wanting to face those things you would be expected to do if you were fully well. When we ignore the reasons for not wanting to get well, and they are almost always subtle and hidden, they become more deeply entrenched as the illness becomes chronic.

The man's response to Jesus is, in effect, "It's not my fault that I can't get to the water in time!" Jesus accepts that response and says very simply, "Stand up, take your mat and walk." Though it must have been shocking to hear those words after so many years of coping with a chronic condition and the frustration of never getting to the pool on time, the man responds with trust and hope. He is instantly healed, takes up his mat, and leaves without even knowing who it is that has healed him.

This is a conflict narrative as well as a healing story. Jesus is criticized for healing on the Sabbath, as was frequently the case, and this becomes an occasion for Jesus to make it clear that human wholeness is a much higher priority than a scrupulous observance of the law. Both the healing and the controversy that follows clearly reveal the will of God, the deep yearning of God for this man and for every person—that they be whole. The law, like health, is never an end in itself but only a means to the greater end of healing others and serving God.

The person doing this exercise should be encouraged to reflect on his or her need for healing. It may be a physical problem, an emotional wound, or a spiritual struggle. The problem should be chronic. It need not be something major, but it should be something that the person has wrestled with for a long time.

Guided Imagery

Give yourself permission to relax . . . releasing the tensions with which you have burdened your body during the waking hours . . . releasing the tensions coming from the normal physical activity needed to keep you erect, keep you alert, keep you mobile, keep you attentive . . . releasing the tensions coming from the stress you've felt about what you've had to do, how fast you've had to do it, and how well you've had to do it . . . letting all of that tension melt away, from the top of your forehead down through the whole of your body . . . letting the tension flow from your body like water flowing gently from the roof of a house . . . breathing in fresh air and energy . . . breathing out tension and fatigue . . . feeling safe and secure in this place . . . allowing yourself to move gently and safely down the well of your inner being, there to enter an underground stream of living water that links you to all those in this place who, like you, are in need of healing. (*Pause for 30 seconds*)

Imagine that you and a group of other people in need of healing are by a pool of water that is known for its healing power. It may be a pool like the one you picture at

Bethesda, but it could just as easily be a pool located at a healing spa you are familiar with or a pool that you create in your mind's eye right now. (*Pause for 15 seconds*)

Scan your inner awareness for anything in your body or your life that is chronically ill or malfunctioning. It may be something physical, but it could be a relationship or an emotional wound from the past that will not heal. Choose something you have struggled with for a long time but that continues to fester and cause distress. I will give you a moment to identify the dis–ease from which you yearn to be delivered. (*Pause for 1 minute*)

Notice some of the other people who are around the pool, people like you in need of healing, some of them clearly in worse shape than you are but others not as bad. All of you are there because the water in this pool has extraordinary healing power, but you also know that only one person at a time can benefit from it. Imagine what it would be like if you were in competition with all these people for healing; you are quite sure that some of them have a distinct advantage over you, perhaps because they have more money or influence or are more deserving or have stronger faith. How does that make you feel about yourself? About the others in the group? About a world in which some are healed and others are not? About a God who either makes it that way or allows it to happen? (*Pause for 30 seconds*)

As you reflect on these things, imagine that you see Jesus approaching you. He walks past all of the others and comes directly to you, sitting down beside you. Looking intently into your eyes, he asks, "Do you want to be made well?" Give yourself some time before you answer. It's an important question, otherwise Jesus wouldn't have asked it. I will give you a moment to reflect on the question. Be sure to ask yourself why you might not want to be made well, and jot down those reasons with a word or phrase that character-izes your resistance. (*Pause for 2 minutes*)

However you have responded to the question of Jesus, begin a conversation with him about your request for heal-ing and whether you really want to be healed, allowing the dialogue to go back and forth until you feel that the issue has been resolved in your mind. As the dialogue begins, record it in writing, both what Jesus says and how you respond. Let the writing flow spontaneously, without effort on your part and without questioning what comes into your mind. (*Allow 5 minutes for writing*)

After you have drawn your conversation with Jesus to a close, imagine Jesus leading you over to the pool. Let your imagination determine how the story unfolds from this point on. What does Jesus say about the water? What does he do with the water? What does he ask you to do? Experience it fully, all of the physical feelings as well as your emotional response. (*Pause for 1 minute*) Now respond to what Jesus has done and said to you. Do or say whatever seems natural to you. (*Pause for 1 minute*) Draw this story to a close, and, as you feel ready, write for a few moments out of the experience, letting the words express what you spontaneously feel and think without any second-guessing or critical assessment. (*Allow 5 minutes for writing*)

Healing of the Man Born Blind

JOHN 9:1–41

Introduction

Like many of the other healings of Jesus, this one is surrounded by controversy. In the verse immediately preceding the narrative, John tells us that some of the Jews took up stones to throw at him, so incensed were they by Jesus' claim to be greater than Abraham. Thus it is not surprising that the Pharisees are ready with their criticism when Jesus heals the man who was born blind. The healing was done on the Sabbath, as were other healings of Jesus, and that was reason enough to condemn him. What is it about healing that evokes antagonism from religious leaders? Healing has triggered controversy throughout the history of the church, as is evident in the opposition to Christian Science, faith healing, the charismatic movement, and even ancient traditional rituals like the laying on of hands and anointing with oil.

Though the disciples do not question Jesus' authority to heal, they seem to imply that the blind man in the story deserves his condition when they ask, "Rabbi, who sinned, this man or his parents, that he was born blind?" The issue they raise is the relationship between sin and sickness, and the way they ask the question indicates that they believe there is a direct correlation between this man's condition and the judgment of God. That belief is as common today as it was then. Often the first question people ask when they get sick is, Why is God punishing me? What have I done to deserve this?

Jesus does not accept the premise of the question, that the man's blindness is a result of either his or his parents' sin. Instead Jesus says that the man's blindness is an occasion for showing the mercy of God. A helpful principle underlies Jesus' response to the disciples' question. Don't get entangled in conjectures about why a person gets sick. Focus your attention on what can be done about it. It's in the doing of mercy that you will see God at work. And so Jesus heals the man, who responds by giving glory to God and becoming a disciple. So here, as elsewhere, the healing is total. Sight is restored both physically and spiritually.

Jesus uses a unique method to heal the man. After spitting on the ground and making some clay, Jesus applies it to the man's eyes and tells him to wash in the pool of Siloam. This requires a tangible act of faith that goes beyond waiting for something to happen, such as when Elisha tells Naaman to bathe in the river to heal his leprosy (2 Kings 5). The same test of faith is present for the man in John's story. He passes the test, for he sees beyond the man who healed him to the God who saved him.

The purpose of the first of the two exercises for this healing story is to help us identify with the blind man. Most of the time we talk about the stories in the Bible as something that happened in ancient history and search for spiritual meanings that can be applied to our daily lives. Using guided imagery to become a participant in the story can deepen its meaning, foster concern for the disabled, and help us to be more conscious of the caring presence of Christ in struggles with adversity. A simple but revealing way to prepare for the first exercise is to have members of the group walk around in the room with their eyes closed for a few moments before the exercise.

The purpose of the second exercise is to help us reflect on our own disabilities (large or small), how we are coping with them, and the difference the healing presence of Christ can make.

Neither of these exercises should be used in a manner that would foster hope for a physical cure in those who have an organic condition that is irreversible, such as blindness marked by tissue damage so severe that recovery of sight would literally be a new creation.

EXERCISE 1, THE MAN BORN BLIND

Guided Imagery

Make yourself comfortable and relax as fully as you can, letting your body become as limp as an old rag doll. Let all tension drain from your body, beginning with your forehead and facial muscles . . . letting the muscles in your face, including your jaw, become loose and limp . . . feeling the tension drain from the neck and the shoulders, where so much accumulated stress is stored . . . relaxing your arms and wrists and fingers, all the strain and tension slipping away from your whole body, away from your chest and abdomen and down through your legs and feet . . . letting all of the tension drain out of your body and into the ground until your body is so limp and tension-free that you feel like you are floating gently on a soft cloud.

Close your eyes so that you will not be distracted by anything going on outside you, and more important, so that you will be able to appreciate what it is like not to see. Imagine what it would be like to have lost the ability to see, so that the opening of your eyelids would not be the opening of your eyes. No longer able to see where you are walking. No longer able to look at those whom you love. No longer able to see snow-capped mountains or the shimmering light of the moon reflected on the waters of a lake or an ocean. Imagine the differences in your day-to-day activities: getting home from this place, doing your job, relating to people, buying groceries. Take a moment to let yourself move deeply into the condition of blindness, beyond an "as if" condition to the condition itself. (*Pause for 2 minutes*)

With your mind's eye, the only eye by which the blind can see, picture yourself as a contemporary of Jesus residing in Jerusalem. Locate yourself outside the temple, where you can hear inside the temple gates a heated argument between Jesus and some other people. Remembering that you are blind, let an image of that scene form in your mind. Imagine where you might be standing or sitting, how you might have been dressed, and whether you are alone or with others . . . . . You are aware of a commotion as Jesus and his disciples pass by, and your ears are quick to pick up a question that the disciples are asking Jesus about you. "Rabbi, who sinned, this man or his parents, that he was born blind?" Imagine what it would be like to hear that question asked about you but not directed to you, and asked by people you cannot even see. How does it make you feel to be treated like an object of idle curiosity? And how would you answer the question if it were directed to you: "Who sinned, you or your parents, that you were born blind?" Does the question make you angry? Or have you asked the question yourself, "What have I done to deserve this? Why are you judging me so harshly, O God?" I will allow you time to reflect on the relationship between sin and sickness in your life. (*Pause for 2 minutes*)

Jesus says: "Neither this man nor his parents sinned; he was born blind so that God's works might be revealed in him." Still talking about you rather than to you, still an object lesson rather than a person who has needs. But Jesus refuses to blame you or anyone else for your blindness. Does that surprise you? And is there hope born out of promise when he says you are to be an occasion for showing the mercy of God? Might it be that Jesus has seen your need, is responsive to your need, is willing to heal you?

With a finely developed sense of intuition, you are aware that Jesus has turned his attention directly to you. Feel his presence directly in front of you. What are you expecting Jesus to do? Will he offer you words of comfort to bear your burden with patience and courage? Will he assure you that you are not being punished by God but rather being given the opportunity to witness to your faith out of your affliction? Dare you hope that he might restore your sight? Take a moment to reflect on what you would expect in such a situation. (*Pause for 1 minute*)

As you wait and think and pray, you feel the touch of Jesus placing clay on your eyes, and hear him say, "Go, wash in the pool of Siloam." What might this mean? Why the clay on your eyes? Why wash in a pool? Those questions, born out of deeply conditioned feelings of suspicion and mistrust, are gradually replaced by other deeply felt questions: Do you trust him? Are you willing to do what he asks? What might be expected of you if your sight is restored? Take a moment to respond in your innermost self to the words and actions of Jesus. (*Pause for 1 minute*)

Picture yourself going to the pool and bathing in it. Imagine how you would get there and what you would be feeling along the way . . . . . Feel the water of the pool as you step into it. Gradually move into the pool until the water is up to your waist. Reach down into the water with your hands and cover your face with the water, and then immerse yourself completely in that water, rubbing your hands over your eyes. As you emerge from the water, imagine opening your eyes and seeing the world for the very first time: seeing those who have cared for you, seeing the water and how it moves, seeing the blue sky and fleecy clouds, seeing animals and trees, and seeing a reflection of yourself in the water—all for the first time. (*Pause for 1 minute*)

As the experience deepens and as you feel ready, write what you are feeling and thinking about the experience of having your sight restored. (*Allow 10–15 minutes for writing*)

EXERCISE 2, CHRONIC DISABILITY

Guided Imagery

Make yourself comfortable and relax as fully as you can, letting your body become as limp as an old rag doll. Let all tension drain from your body, beginning with your forehead and facial muscles . . . letting the muscles in your face, including your jaw, become loose and limp . . . feeling the tension drain from the neck and the shoulders, where so much accumulated stress is stored . . . relaxing your arms and wrists and fingers, all the strain and tension slipping away from your whole body, away from your chest and abdomen and down through your legs and feet . . . letting all of the tension drain out of your body and into the ground until your body is so limp and tension-free that you feel like you are floating gently on a soft cloud.

Let an image form of yourself as physically, emotionally, or spiritually disabled. Choose a disability that you have struggled with for a long time and magnify it many times over until it becomes the major preoccupation of your life. It need not be a physical disability or even a major problem at present, but something that limits you in a significant way. Let the disability become the image of you, not something that you have but something that you are. Imagine others staring at you and seeing only your disability, pointing to you and talking to each other about you. Look into the mirror and see not yourself but your disability. As you gaze at this image of yourself as disabled, finish the following sentences with whatever comes into your mind: The adjective that best describes me is . . . . . The way I feel about myself is . . . . . What I need is . . . . . More than anything else I wish that . . . . .

Imagine yourself in some public place, perhaps in church or out on the street, your disability obvious to everyone around you. Jesus passes by this place. One of the people who has been staring at you stops Jesus, points at you, and asks him a question. Though you can't hear the question, you know it's about you and your disability. Without answering the question, Jesus comes directly to you. Imagine him approaching you now. Look into his face. Let his eyes meet yours. What do you see there? What do you need most from him? What do you expect from him? Ask Jesus anything you want about your disability . . . why you have it . . . what it says about you . . . how you're coping with it. After you've asked Jesus what you wish to ask him about your disability, listen carefully to what he has to say to you about that disability. (*Pause for 2 minutes*)

Now imagine Jesus addressing himself directly to your disability. This can take any form that your imagination suggests. If your disability is a physical one, it might be that Jesus will touch the place or places on your body where the disability manifests itself, or perhaps rub oil on it. If the disability is emotional or spiritual, it may be that he will take your hands into his as he talks to you about it. Let yourself feel the presence of Jesus and allow the scene to unfold naturally. (*Pause for 1 minute*)

Now imagine Jesus taking you by the hand and leading you to a beautiful pool of water. With your hand still in his, he leads you into the pool and with a seashell pours water over your head. As the water flows over you, you are reminded of the healing waters of your baptism. The years between your baptism and the present fade away, and you know that you are God's child, made whole through the healing waters of baptism and promised the eternal love and care of God. In your mind's eye imagine the water of this pool flowing over and around and through your disability, bringing wholeness where there was brokenness, harmony and balance where there was discord and tension, bringing healing that fills you totally with the awareness of being God's beloved child. Take a moment to experience the healing of your disability in whatever form that might take. As the experience deepens, and when you feel ready, let your pen spontaneously express your feelings and thoughts without critical analysis or scrutiny. (*Allow 10–15 minutes for writing*)

Healing the Woman
with the Crippled Back

LUKE 13:10–17

Introduction

The story on which this exercise is based is one of the few stories where a woman is singled out for healing. There are only two other clear examples of Jesus healing a woman, Peter's mother-in-law and the woman who had frequent hemorrhaging. All the other stories of healing are about men. Though women can identify with men who are healed and men can identify with the woman in this story, I think women will find this exercise particularly helpful. I say that not only because she is a woman but also because of her condition. "She was bent over and was quite unable to stand up straight." Identifying with this condition will be easier for women because they suffer more than men from osteoporosis, a bone disease that often results in a curvature of the spine. Even more significant is the posture of being bent over, which is symbolic of submission, and Jesus' suggestion that her condition was the result of oppression by the powers of evil, an oppression women can link to many of their ailments. More than physical healing is called for, as is obvious when Jesus heals her: "Woman, you are set free from your ailment."

This healing is about liberation. It happens on the Sabbath, which is a day of liberation from work and a day on which the Jews reflected on their liberation from a land of bondage. Sunday is our Sabbath, the day when we reflect on the paschal mystery and celebrate our liberation from death. What better place than the synagogue to heal and what better day than the Sabbath to do it? This is how Jesus responds to the critic who *keeps saying* to the crowd, not to the woman, "There are six days on which work ought to be done; come on one of the other six days of the week to be healed, and not on the Sabbath day." Liberation is at the heart of worship, liberation from our ailments as well as the spirit of oppression that contributes to our ailments, such as a person in a position of power arguing that we shouldn't be healed.

It would be advisable to read the story in Luke before doing the exercise if you or the persons doing the exercise are not familiar with it. The exercise will begin with an experiential participation in the original story, after which those doing the exercise will be asked to substitute a personal ailment for the crippled back of the woman in the story.

Guided Imagery

Be aware of your body and note any places of tension that you find there: perhaps a stiffness in your neck or shoulder or back; perhaps a tightness in your abdomen, like a knot that needs to be unraveled; maybe just an overall feeling of tension. Wherever you are aware of tension in your body, consciously let go of it and feel it drain away. Let all of the tension within you flow down and out of your body like newly melted snow flowing down a mountain stream.

Pay attention to your breathing and its natural rhythm . . . attuning yourself to that rhythm and becoming more and more relaxed . . . letting your mind be drained of worry as your body is drained of tension . . . letting any distracting thoughts float free in your consciousness, giving them no special heed . . . concentrating only on your breathing . . . breathing in the Spirit of God . . . breathing out all worry and tension . . . feeling more and more relaxed as you release all the tensions and worries that have been burdening you. (*Pause for 30 seconds*)

In your mind's eye, imagine yourself with a chronic back condition that keeps you constantly stooped over. As an aid to your imagination, assume that position now in the chair where you are sitting and keep that position until you are given further instructions. Imagine what it would be like never to be able to straighten your back again. Picture yourself leaving this room, driving your car, and engaged in any other activity that would be a normal routine for you. (*Pause for 30 seconds*)

What is it that is going on in your life right now that has you stooped over, as if you were carrying a heavy burden? Is it some physical infirmity, perhaps a chronic condition that has crippled you? Is it a spiritual condition that has left you bent and burdened, such as a relationship in which you've been badly treated or a job in which you've received little personal or professional respect? Take a moment to identify what it is in your life that leaves you stooped in body, mind, and spirit. (*Pause for 1 minute*)

Are you aware of feeling oppressed or being victimized? Do you see any connection between the ailment that you have identified and other forces of evil in your life, maybe even a direct causal connection? With the aid of your memory and your imagination, trace the history of this ailment as it unfolded from its earliest beginnings to what it is today. (*Pause for 1 minute*)

Still in a stooped position, imagine yourself entering a synagogue of ancient Israel. It is the Sabbath, and you have gone there for instruction and worship. As you enter, you notice that the one who is teaching is Jesus. It is your intention to slip quietly to the back of those who are listening, because you are eager to hear this man who is being called a great teacher and healer. Jesus immediately notices you and, to your surprise and embarrassment, asks you to come to him. Imagine yourself working your way to the front of the group, stooped over and aware that people are staring at you and annoyed at the interruption. (*Pause for 15 seconds*)

From your stooped position, look up at the face of Jesus. What do you see there? Is he annoyed because you interrupted his teaching? Do you suppose that he's about to use you as an object lesson for one of his stories? Given what you see in Jesus' face, what do you expect from him? What do you want from him? Everybody else and everything else fades into the background as your attention is riveted firmly on the face of Jesus. Take a moment to deepen the experience of being invited by Jesus to come to him and waiting expectantly for what he will say or do next. (*Pause for 30 seconds*)

Imagine your surprise at hearing these words from Jesus: "You are set free from your ailment." Set free, liberated from something that you've been burdened with for eighteen years. Is it possible? Can this be true after all these years? Still surprised by Jesus' words, feel his hands being laid on that portion of your back which is bent and stiff. As you straighten your back, imagine what it would be like to do that for the first time in eighteen years. As your back straightens, feel the burden of the ailment you have identified being lifted from your shoulders. "You are set free from your ailment." Imagine yourself standing up straight and being able to look people in the eye. As you look into the eyes of Jesus, what is it that you want to say or do? (*Pause for 20 seconds*) As you look into the eyes of the leader who kept saying to the crowds that you shouldn't be healed, what is it that you want to say to him? (*Pause for 20 seconds*) As you look into the eyes of the crowd of people who are there, what is it that you want to say to them? (*Pause for 20 seconds*)

As you feel ready, express your thoughts and feelings in writing about the experience of being set from an ailment that you have suffered with for many years. Let the writing be spontaneous, without any effort on your part to guide your reflections in a particular direction or to evaluate what you are thinking and feeling. (*Allow 10–15 minutes for writing*)

Chapter 3

Exercises for Meeting Spiritual Needs

In recent years literature on the philosophy of health care has emphasized care of the whole person. Even physicians who are deeply committed to the scientific objectivity of the traditional medical model recognize the value of whole-person health care. What that means, for the most part, is greater attention to psychosocial factors that affect both the causes of illness and the care of persons who are ill. Until recently the spiritual dimension of health care has received little attention, except from the clergy, who have always visited the sick. But many sick people are unchurched and thus untreated as far as spiritual care is concerned. That is changing, with more and more hospitals including a chaplaincy department and more and more medical professionals becoming sensitive to the spiritual needs of patients.

Spiritual needs are needs of the human spirit for meaning and purpose, for forgiveness, reassurance, acceptance, hope, peace, and for giving thanks. These are but a few suggestions of the kinds of needs that can be considered spiritual. They are universal, not just for those who consider themselves to be religious. They are needs that can be met on both a horizontal and a vertical plane. On the horizontal level are family, friends, health care givers, and many others. But for most people that is not enough, especially in crisis situations. At such times religion, the vertical plane, becomes the primary resource for meeting spiritual needs. For Christians this means turning to the healing presence of God as experienced most fully in Christ the Healer.

Spiritual needs are not only common to all people, they are present throughout the life cycle, in both health and illness, good times and bad, stress and calm, success and failure. In good times we are often unaware of our spiritual needs, usually because they are being met in quite ordinary ways. In bad times, such as facing serious loss, spiritual needs often surface to awareness, either because they are not being met as before or because their intensity has increased dramatically. If I incur an illness that makes it impossible for me to work, for instance, the meaning of my life is called into question. At the onset of a life-threatening illness, the need for reassurance and hope will rapidly escalate. At such times those needs are at least as important as psychosocial and physical needs.

In my experience most care givers feel less adequate in meeting spiritual needs than either physical or psychosocial needs. The exercises in this chapter are designed to help those who provide spiritual care to patients: clergy, health care professionals, family, and friends. They can be used in groups, in one-to-one care-giving relationships, or in private as a form of spiritual self-care. If used as a form of spiritual care in one-to-one relationships, which is their chief value, the care giver should encourage the person doing the exercise to respond verbally at appropriate places. This will require a more flexible use of the material in the exercise.

Self-care is as appropriate in meeting spiritual needs as it is in meeting any other kind of need. The experience of being cared for is likely to be deepened when it comes from another, not only because of the healing power in relationships, but also because one does not have to be both care giver and receiver at the same time. However, such a care giver is not always available, and sometimes not even desired. Some people are more comfortable in providing spiritual care for themselves within the safety and privacy of their personal relationship to God.

Identifying Spiritual Needs

The purpose of this brief exercise is to help people identify their spiritual needs. As indicated above, most people are more likely to be conscious of physical and emotional needs than spiritual needs, both in themselves and others. The exercise can be used as a training tool for professional or lay counselors or health care workers who want to become more sensitive to the spiritual needs of the patients they care for. It can also be used by recovery groups; addiction is often related to unmet spiritual needs. Since spiritual needs are part of normal experience in health as well as illness, this could be used as a wellness exercise in a group that has as one of its goals the nurturing of spirituality. Finally, the exercise can be used privately for nurturing one's own spirituality.

Spend some time in reflecting on the idea of spiritual needs and compiling a list of them before beginning the exercise. Some space for writing should be left between the listing of categories. If you're leading a group, discuss with them the universality of spiritual needs and the different ways they are met, noting especially the difference between secular and religious ways of meeting spiritual needs. The listing of spiritual needs should be personal, though there will likely be agreement on the broad categories from which a personal list can be constructed: meaning and purpose, forgiveness, relatedness, reassurance, acceptance, peace, hope, gratitude, self-esteem, control, dignity, and personal worth. Some of those categories overlap, and more items could be added.

Guided Imagery

Close your eyes or keep them focused on one place in the room so that you can pay attention to what is going on inside you rather than on what is happening outside you. We take too little time for ourselves, our needs—especially our spiritual needs—and what we are feeling and thinking deep within the core of our being. Concentrate on your breathing . . . breathing in . . . and breathing out . . . sensing the inner rhythm of your body, your self . . . feeling the peace that comes with adjusting your whole being to the rhythm of your breathing . . . letting all the problems that you have been wrestling with slip away from your consciousness . . . allowing yourself to come to rest . . . letting the thoughts that pop into your mind simply float away like balloons drifting toward the sky. Be aware of how many of your needs are met daily without much concern on your part—food to eat and clothing to wear, fresh air to breathe and clean water to drink, a safe place to live. So many ways that you have been blessed, so many needs that have been met. Feel the goodness of being alive at this very moment and blessed with so many of the gifts of life.

Direct your thoughts and feelings to your spiritual needs. Reflect on the spiritual needs that you have identified for yourself, opening your eyes just enough to scan the list if you need to remember what you wrote. Let that list serve as a grid through which you can filter your experience and identify the spiritual needs that are most prominent in your life right now. As you reflect on each of those needs, like meaning and purpose, identify experiences that have made you conscious of this need and then jot down a word or phrase that will remind you of this experience. There may be as many as five or six experiences for some needs and none for others. Don't pass judgment on your spontaneous selection of experiences by asking, Why did I think of that? or That's not important. Trust your intuitive grasp of what is deep-down important, and simply record what you're aware of. I will give you a few moments to record the experiences you remember as you reflect on the spiritual needs that are prominent in your life. (*Allow 3–5 minutes for completion*)

Looking over the list of spiritual needs and the notations you have made, select one need that awakens the greatest intensity of feeling in you. In your mind's eye, enter into that need, letting yourself become that need for a few moments. Reenter one of the experiences when you were particularly aware of that need, and feel what you felt then.

How would you describe the need from within your experience of it? What exactly is it that you need, and who can supply it? Is it OK to have this need? Or is it hard for you to admit it to yourself, to others, to God? Are you able to ask for what you need? Or do you expect others to observe that need and respond to it without your asking? After you have taken the time to enter deeply into this spiritual need and to experience it from within, express what you are feeling and thinking in writing. Begin with these words: "What I need is . . . . ." Let your pen simply be a medium for what comes from within. Don't analyze or critique what you are experiencing. Don't be concerned about sentence construction or writing style. Don't feel rushed. Experience the need deeply before you try to give expression to it in writing. (*Allow 5–10 minutes for writing*)

Returning to the inner world of your experience, reflect for a moment on the religious dimension of this need. Is it also a need in relation to God, perhaps particularly in relation to God? Do you see your faith as a resource in meeting your spiritual need? Would prayer help? What would you pray for? For God to do something? For the strength and courage to do something yourself? Is there any portion of Scripture that comes to mind as a resource for dealing with this need? Take a few moments to reflect on your need within the framework of your relationship to God. As you feel ready, write whatever best expresses the felt sense of your faith in response to this need. Perhaps it may take the form of a prayer or a meditation or a dialogue with God in which you write down what you want to say to God and then listen for what God would say in return, letting the dialogue flow back and forth. Use whatever form of expression seems most natural to you. (*Allow 5–10 minutes for writing*)

Receiving Spiritual Care

Introduction

This exercise is designed primarily for persons being trained to become sensitive to spiritual needs and to provide spiritual care. I'm not thinking so much of professionals in spiritual care, such as the clergy, as I am of laypersons who want to become more sensitive to the spiritual needs of others. This exercise, as well as others in this chapter, can be a resource for the training of Stephen ministers or other lay counselors who have become primary providers of spiritual care in many congregations. It could also be used in a congregational workshop on spiritual needs and health care, to which health care workers could be given a special invitation. Since every Christian has opportunities to provide spiritual care to others, this exercise can be profitably used by any layperson, privately or in groups.

A person who provides care for others must know how to receive it. It is harder for most people to receive care than to give it. This exercise will lead you through an experience of receiving care from another. In the process, you will be able to discern points of resistance, types of spiritual need, ways of caring that are most effective, and ways of communicating the goodness and mercy of God. Though the primary purpose of the exercise is to train people as care givers, it is obvious that in doing the exercise they will develop a keener awareness of their own need for spiritual care.

If this exercise is used with a training group or in a workshop, it should be followed by a discussion. That process might begin with groups of two or three sharing their experience of the exercise, followed by sharing in the larger group. Such a discussion might be concluded with a brainstorming session on general principles of providing spiritual care.

Guided Imagery

Letting the chair beneath you bear your full weight, make yourself as comfortable as you can . . . listening only to the sound of my voice as I guide you to a quiet place inside yourself . . . letting all other sounds and all other distracting thoughts fade into the background . . . knowing that this exercise on being cared for is the most important thing that you have to do right now . . . becoming aware of your breathing in its smooth and natural rhythm . . . always in perfect harmony with the rest of your body . . . breathing in the breath of life, the breath that God first breathed into Adam . . . breathing in the Spirit of God, who brings healing into your life . . . breathing out fear and anything that keeps you from being the child of God that you are . . . sitting in quiet and calm . . . aware only of the sound of my voice and the gentle movement of your breathing, breathing that brings peace and quiet and readiness for healing . . . waiting for the movement of the Spirit of God deep within you . . . aware of seeing with more than your eye, of hearing with more than your ear, of knowing with more than your mind.

Take a few moments in the quiet of this place to reflect back over the years of your life to some of the personal crises you have faced. It may have been a physical illness or an accident. It may have been the loss of a parent or someone else whom you loved. The crisis may have been a loss of faith. It may have been something that turned out to be quite minor but seemed to be a huge crisis to you at the time, forcing you to use all of your coping skills and perhaps develop some new ones. Let about five or six such crises surface in your mind as you, in your mind's eye, retrace the years. Imagine yourself floating down the stream of your life and letting memories emerge spontaneously. Don't analyze or second-guess your intuitions by asking, Why this crisis? Though you may not have thought about it for years, trust your intuition to identify what is important. I'll give you a moment of quiet reflection for this journey through time. (*Pause for 2 minutes*)

Having identified a number of significant crises in your life, choose one about which you still have strong feelings—perhaps because it was fairly recent, or maybe because it had such deep ramifications. (*Pause for 15 seconds*) Reenter that experience with the aid of your memory and imagination. Where were you at the time it happened?

What were some of the circumstances that led up to the crisis? What made the experience so difficult for you? How did you cope with the crisis? What were some of the weaknesses with your way of coping? What were some of the strengths? What role did your faith play in coping with the crisis? Did you turn to others for help? What difference did that make? Let your reflections flow smoothly and naturally without judgment or criticism on your part. I'll give you a moment to experience your need to be cared for by others and by God. (*Pause for 1 minute*)

Reflect for a moment on the people who cared for you in that crisis. Who was there? Who was the person who offered you the most support? Perhaps there were a number of key people. What was it that he or she did that was so helpful? What particular needs of yours were met? Perhaps there wasn't anyone there. If not, who would you like to have been there, and what kind of help would you be looking for? . . . . . What were your spiritual needs and how well were they met? . . . Did you want anyone to offer you spiritual care? If not in memory, then in your mind's eye imagine a friend, a nurse, perhaps a counselor offering to read a portion of Scripture, whatever would be meaningful to you . . . . . What is your reaction to that offer? Are you surprised? gratified? upset? embarrassed? Now imagine a friend holding your hand and offering a prayer for strength and courage and inner peace. Does that seem appropriate? Or does it seem like an invasion of your privacy? I'll give you a moment to reflect on what it is like for you to receive spiritual care from someone else. (*Pause for 1 minute*)

Turn your attention to the present. Consider how well prepared you are for meeting whatever crises life may have in store for you and how willing you are to ask for help or accept help in your time of need. After a moment or two of interior reflection, write whatever comes to you when you say to yourself: If I were to get seriously ill in the near future, what I would need and want most from those who are taking care of me is . . . . . (*Allow 5–10 minutes for writing*)

Forgiveness

Forgiveness is without question one of the primary spiritual needs. If sin is understood as estrangement from self, others, the world, and God, then forgiveness is constantly needed for the restoration of those relationships. Those who minister to the sick, especially the clergy, have long known how prominent this need is in times of illness. Frequently persons who are sick see a connection between their illness and their sin, often a causal connection. Every spiritual care giver has heard the agonized question, What have I done to deserve this? Rather than trying to talk the person out of the feeling of judgment that prompts the question, it is better to respond to the need for forgiveness—without, of course, reinforcing the misguided theology that makes a cause and effect relationship between sin and illness.

The exercise that follows can be done in a variety of ways. It could be used privately by making a tape recording of the exercise. That way you both speak and hear the word of forgiveness that is the promise of the gospel. The most profitable use of the exercise can be made in a person-to-person relationship where a pastor, a health care giver, or some other fellow Christian, such as a lay counselor, serves as a guide. Finally, this exercise might possibly be used as a corporate confession and absolution at the beginning of a worship service. That would require some adaptation of what follows as well as careful consideration about whether this would be an appropriate use of guided imagery. While helpful for many, it may impede rather than facilitate the confession of some.

The following exercise not only structures the time set aside for confession, it also enables the confession to be more concrete and experiential. A formal confession of sins divorced from experience and followed by a ritual pronouncement of the forgiveness of sins in general will not meet the spiritual hunger for a personal word of forgiveness that is for me. Imagery can help many people (not all) to connect a ritual of asking for and receiving forgiveness to their personal experience.

There are five parts to this imagery exercise. The first two deal with personal relationships that call for both forgiving others and being forgiven by them. The next two parts deal with concrete deeds of commission and omission that are not directly related to personal relationships. The last part deals with the person's faith.

It is not necessary to include all five parts in every use of this exercise, though all five dimensions are important components of a general confession of sins. The exercise can be abridged by combining either the first two parts or the second two parts. This exercise lends itself well to writing, which can be included at the end of each section if the time and place of usage allow for it. If used with a person who is feeling the effects of illness, the exercise should be kept short and exclude writing.

Guided Imagery

Close your eyes so that you can turn inward and see yourself rather than seeing others and the world around you . . . readying yourself for reflecting on the story of your life in relation to God, to yourself, to others, to the whole world. Pay attention to your breathing as a way of moving inward, and with each breath feel yourself becoming more relaxed and more secure within the world of your inner experience . . . letting your breathing become slower and deeper . . . paying no heed to thoughts that may come into your mind, allowing them to drift aimlessly out of your consciousness . . . breathing evenly and deeply, and with each breath becoming more deeply aware of the world within, with your mind attuned to every nuance of thought and feeling, as you prepare to reflect on the story of your life in the light of your faith. (*Pause for 20 seconds*)

Jesus was a friend of sinners. He told the story of a father's love for a son who had wasted his life. He intervened on behalf of a woman who was about to be stoned for adultery. He forgave those who had placed him on a cross. In your mind's eye, imagine that Jesus is with you now, listening to your story with the same love and compassion he showed to others.

In the presence of this loving Jesus, let a picture of some person you have wronged surface in your mind. With the aid of your imagination, relive the story of what happened between you and this person. (*Pause for 1 minute*) What is it that you did or failed to do that makes you feel guilty? . . . What are the feelings that led up to this occasion? . . . Are you able to anticipate the consequences that you know resulted from your behavior? . . . Are you aware of feelings of guilt? . . . As you are ready, express whatever is in your heart to Jesus and then wait for his response. (*Pause for 1–2 minutes*) Imagine what might be possible now in your relationship to the person you wronged. Don't force any particular outcome. It may be unrealistic to expect a change in your relationship. Trust your inner sense of what is possible, and let images of that unfold naturally. (*Pause for 1–2 minutes*) (*If there is sufficient time, follow the same procedure for others who may have been wronged.*)

Still in the presence of Jesus, bring to mind someone whom you need to forgive, someone who has wronged you. With the aid of your imagination, relive the story of what happened between you and this person. (*Pause for 1 minute*) What is it that she or he did or failed to do? . . . What feelings does this evoke in you? . . . Are you able to sense what she or he is feeling and why? . . . Are you feeling any guilt for your part in what is happening between you? . . . As you are ready, express whatever is in your heart to Jesus, and then wait for his response. (*Pause for 1–2 minutes*) Imagine what might be possible now in your relationship to the person who has wronged you. Don't force any particular outcome. It may be unrealistic to expect a change in your relationship. Trust your inner sense of what is possible, and let images of that unfold naturally. (*Pause for 1–2 minutes*) (*If there is sufficient time, direct the persons to follow the same procedure for others who may have wronged them.*)

Still in the presence of Jesus, let images surface in your mind of things that you have done not directly related to other persons for which you feel shame or guilt, perhaps a sin against yourself or against the environment. As each picture forms, however vague it may be, silently pray, "Lord Jesus, have mercy." It is not necessary to dwell on any of the pictures that form in your mind. Simply be aware of them and ask for Jesus' mercy. When it seems that you have completed this process, imagine that Jesus forgives you in any way that seems appropriate—perhaps simply through what he says, but perhaps also through what he does, such as placing his hands on your head and making the sign of the cross on your forehead. (*Pause for 1 minute*)

Still in the presence of Jesus, let images form in your mind of things you should have done but failed to do and for which you feel shame or guilt. As each picture forms, however vague it may be, silently pray, "Lord Jesus, have mercy." It is not necessary to dwell on any of the pictures that arise. Simply be aware of them and plead for mercy. When it seems that you have completed this process, imagine once again that Jesus forgives you in any way that seems appropriate. (*Pause for 1 minute*)

Speak with Jesus now about things you have done and things you have failed to do that have been harmful to your life of faith. Search for an image that will express the condition of your faith right now, which might be anything from a soaring eagle to a broken reed. After you have talked with Jesus about your life of faith, listen carefully to his response. (*Pause for 2 minutes*)

As you are ready, come away from your meeting with Jesus and reorient yourself to this place, cleansed and refreshed in your spirit. Do that slowly. Be gentle with yourself.

Hope in the Midst of Adversity

Hope is tied to the assurance that there is a future that holds promise; our hope is rooted deep in promise. There are limits to the hope that can be generated on a purely horizontal plane, limits to what medicine can offer and to what any human community can finally promise. Christian hope is rooted in the promise of the gospel that nothing can separate us from the love of God in Christ, not even the power of death, whose dark shadow puts every medical claim to victory in proper perspective.

The following exercise is written for a person who is overwhelmed by adversity and feeling somewhat desperate because there is no obvious way to escape it. It may be a person who is seriously ill, but it may also be someone who is confronted by a personal or social problem for which there appears to be no solution, such as drug dependence. The exercise will be appropriate for anyone for whom hope is flagging on the horizontal plane of life and who looks to God as a source of hope that can be counted on no matter how great the adversity or how hopeless the situation might seem.

Selected verses from Psalm 27 (NRSV) are used as the basis for this exercise. Reading the entire psalm before the exercise is optional. Doing so may help provide a worshipful frame of reference, but the verses of the psalm needed for meditation are contained in the exercise.

Guided Imagery

Be as comfortable as you can in the chair where you are sitting [bed where you are lying] . . . letting your eyes close so that you can focus on your inner experience rather than on what is happening on the outside . . . relaxing the muscles of your body, beginning with the top of your head down to the bottom of your feet . . . letting your troubled spirit become as calm as the sea that was changed from tempest to stillness by a word from Jesus . . . gradually letting the tension fade away until your body feels relaxed and your spirit feels calm . . . resting quietly and calmly . . . letting your breathing come slowly and regularly . . . letting your inner spirit become as calm as a lake that mirrors the woods behind it . . . letting the worries and fears about your illness [adversity] flow from you as you rest quietly in the ever-lasting arms of God . . . finding deep within yourself a center that is a place of quiet and tranquillity far removed from the disorder and disruption that has been generated by this illness [adversity] . . . resting quietly in the arms of God and confident that God is present in the midst of your adversity.

"The Lord is my light and my salvation; whom shall I fear? The Lord is the stronghold of my life; of whom shall I be afraid?" (Ps. 27:1). What is it that you fear most in your present adversity? Let images of what frightens you surface in your mind. Is it fear of abandonment? Fear that something terrible will happen? Fear that you won't be able to cope? Fear of the unknown? Let the images surface spontaneously without any need on your part to evaluate them or make them go away. Simply be a neutral observer of what you fear most, trying to see and understand as clearly as you can what it is that is troubling you. I will give you a moment to complete that process. (*Pause for 1 minute*)

Pulling yourself back from the fears that haunt you, imagine God as the stronghold of your life. That might take the form of your being in the everlasting arms of God. Or you might imagine a secure place, like a fortress, where God's protection is assured. Or some other image may come to you as you meditate on God as the stronghold of your life. (*Pause for 30 seconds*)

From within the security of God as the stronghold of your life, imagine light coming from God fully surrounding the darkness of what you fear and gradually penetrating that darkness until the fear is gone and the only thing you are aware of is the healing light of God around you and in you. (*Pause for 30 seconds*)

"One thing I asked of the Lord, that will I seek after: to live in the house of the Lord all the days of my life, to behold the beauty of the Lord and to inquire in his temple" (Ps. 27:4). To live in the house of the Lord. Imagine such a house, any kind of house you wish, only make it a house with many rooms, as Jesus described it, and one room prepared for you. Imagine yourself in the house of the Lord and surrounded by people whom you love and who love you. Picture a banquet being served in this house with Jesus as the host and you an invited guest. Feel the goodness of being there: the joy, the fellowship, the warmth, the love. (*Pause for 30 seconds*) Whatever pain and suffering may be crowding out the joy in your life right now, let this promise be your hope.

"Hear, O Lord, when I cry aloud, be gracious to me and answer me! 'Come,' my heart says, 'Seek his face.' Your face, Lord, do I seek. Do not hide your face from me" (Ps. 27: 7–9). With the aid of your memory and your imagination, recall the face of one of the first persons who took care of you, whom you regarded as especially nurturing and gracious: a parent, a grandparent, perhaps someone else. Imagine yourself at the age you were then and looking up into that face as she or he leans down to pick you up and hold you. (*Pause for 15 seconds*) Recall the faces of other people who have nurtured you, protected you, strengthened you, and as you recall each face feel the goodness and safety of their presence. (*Pause for 30 seconds*) Recall those faces again, but this time see the face of God in each of those faces, shining on you with a countenance full of grace and peace. (*Pause for 30 seconds*)

"The Lord is my light and my salvation; whom shall I fear? The Lord is the stronghold of my life; of whom shall I be afraid?" (Ps. 27:1). Imagine the light of God, the light of Christ the Healer, all around you and within you, bathing you in its healing and nurturing power. Each time you exhale, silently say these words, "My light and my salvation." With each breath, "My light and my salvation." (*Pause for 2 minutes*)

As you feel ready, gradually return to this place, feeling refreshed in body, mind, and spirit, and full of hope in the promises of God.

Trusting the Providence of God

Introduction

High on the list of spiritual needs in periods of illness or any other personal adversity is reassurance. One of the inevitable effects of adversity is the loss of control and the awareness of vulnerability.

Both psychologically and spiritually, the need for reassurance is rooted in the earliest experiences of our lives as infants. There is no question about the vulnerability of infants or their need for reassurance; just listen to the screams of a terrified child and notice how quickly the fear subsides when the infant is picked up and rocked gently in the arms of its mother. Those of us who grew up in Christian homes learned to trust God in a manner very similar to the way we learned to trust our parents, the one an extension of the other, the vertical and the horizontal closely intertwined. Unfortunately, increased autonomy and less need for reassurance from parents can foster the illusion that we can be equally independent from God. Illness or some other personal tragedy shatters that illusion and makes us aware that we will never outgrow our need for reassurance from God.

Trusting God is the appropriate faith response to our need for reassurance. Trust always has been and always will be the foundational element of faith — foundational in that it is developmentally the earliest formation of faith, and foundational in that it will be the most prominent element of faith in times of crisis. Trust, as hope, is rooted deep in promise. Thus the need for reassurance in times of crisis is the need to hear the promise of the gospel that God will sustain us with the healing presence of his love, from which nothing can separate us.

Throughout Christian history the imagery of a shepherd and his flock has figured prominently in mediating the promise of the gospel to those in need of reassurance. Best known through the Twenty-third Psalm, the image of a shepherd and his flock appears in stained glass windows, Sunday school leaflets, and in a variety of Christian art forms. The image is used regularly by pastors ministering to the sick and dying. The following exercise is based on the imagery of Jesus as the good shepherd in John 10.

This exercise is designed primarily for use in providing personal spiritual care to someone who is ill or experiencing some other form of life crisis. It can be used without adaptation for self-care by recording the exercise and then following its directions. It could be easily adapted for use with recovery groups, grief groups, cancer patients, or other groups with special needs.

Guided Imagery

As the quietness deepens within you, let your eyes close to avoid outside distraction and to focus more clearly on your inner experience. Imagine that you are in a lovely meadow in the springtime, a meadow with a small lake at its center surrounded by wildflowers that seem to be dancing in the warm and gentle breezes. Feel the warmth of the sun, and catch the scent of the flowers in the air. Imagine your favorite birds flying above you, lazily gliding through the sky with wings outstretched, carefree. With the aid of your imagination, find a comfortable place in the green pasture beside the still water of the lake and feel your body relax as you let go of the tensions that have been stored there . . . letting your worries fly away like birds that have been freed from a cage . . . letting the inner stillness wrap itself around your soul . . . becoming aware of how relaxed and peaceful you feel in this meadow . . . letting your breathing come more slowly and evenly . . . feeling your worries and tensions flowing out of you as you exhale, and feeling the Spirit of God filling you each time you inhale . . . tensions flowing out . . . the Spirit of God flowing in . . . becoming more and more relaxed with each breath, more and more in tune with the slow and graceful rhythm of nature that surrounds you in the meadow. (*Pause for 30 seconds*)

Jesus said, "I am the good shepherd. I know my own and my own know me . . . . . My sheep hear my voice. I know them, and they follow me" (John 10:14). Picture Jesus as the good shepherd. As your good shepherd, Jesus knows you, and you know him and follow him. Imagine Jesus saying to you, "I know you, [name], and I am aware of the adversity that you are facing. And you know me and my promise to protect you, sustain you, feed you, and guide you through any and all tribulation." Take a moment to let these words of Jesus penetrate to the deepest recesses of your inner spirit: "I know you, [name], and I am aware of the adversity that you are facing. And you know me and my promise to protect you, sustain you, feed you, and guide you through any and all tribulation." Keep repeating those words of Jesus to yourself, "I know you, and you know me." (*Pause for 1 minute*)

In your mind's eye imagine a flock of sheep grazing peacefully in a meadow when suddenly a wolf appears at the top of a nearby knoll. Sense the terror that sweeps through members of the flock as the wolf stands poised to attack, each intuitively aware of the hopelessness of any defense against this dire threat. Now imagine the wolf poised to attack you. What threat feels like that? A wolf may not be the only effective way to imagine this. If it's death that threatens you, then perhaps a hooded figure would be a better image. Perhaps no image at all will come to mind, only a strongly felt sense of imminent danger. (*Pause for 30 seconds*)

How do you respond to the presence of the wolf in your life? Where do you turn for help? Keep your attention focused on the human resources that you can count on, yourself and those around you. What could you do? What could others do? (*Pause for 30 seconds*) Do you feel safe now? Or is the threat still there, perhaps held at bay but ready to attack at any sign of weakness? Imagine that the threat is bigger than anything you or anyone else could do to stop it. Let yourself experience the terror of that, the terror that comes with the awareness of total vulnerability. (*Pause for 20 seconds*)

Jesus said, "They will never perish. No one will snatch them out of my hand" (John 10:28). Experience the presence of Jesus, the good shepherd, by your side as you once again focus your attention on what threatens you. Imagine Jesus speaking these words directly to you: "You will never perish. No one will snatch you out of my hand." What do you feel as you hear those words? How do you experience the threat with Jesus at your side? He says, "I lay down my life for the sheep" (John 10:15). Imagine Jesus saying these words directly to you: "I lay down my life for you. Nothing can separate you from me and my love." Let yourself experience fully the reassurance of Jesus' presence and his promise to keep you safe, even at the cost of his own life. (*Pause for 30 seconds*)

Jesus said, "I came that they may have life, and have it abundantly" (John 10:10). Imagine Jesus saying those words directly to you: "I come that you may have life, and have it abundantly." What is the abundant life that Jesus has in mind for you? Picture the abundant life; be as concrete as you can in imagining what Jesus wants for you right now and what he promises you for the future. Let those images surface spontaneously from your inner awareness without any effort on your part to make sense of them or have them all fit together. Simply let yourself feel the goodness of the abundant life that Jesus intends for you. (*Pause for 1 minute*)

As you feel ready, gradually come away from this experience and reorient yourself to the here and now, fully assured that the shepherding presence of Jesus comes with you and will remain with you.

Relaxing into the Peace of God

Shalom (peace) is a Hebrew word for greeting. "I wish you peace." It is a ritual greeting that Christians share in the Eucharist. We all yearn for peace. It is a universal spiritual need. Peace generally means absence of conflict, but the broader biblical meaning of shalom is wholeness. "May you be whole, the way God intended you to be." Wholeness has a double meaning. Freedom from sin and illness is the most obvious meaning. But wholeness also means wellness, or integration of body, mind, and spirit. Understood in this broad sense, peace (wholeness) is the most basic and fundamental of all spiritual needs. To receive it from another person, and above all from God, is always a blessing. Chapter 5 includes an exercise on the giving and receiving of a blessing that meets the spiritual need for peace within the context of a personal relationship.

This exercise meets the spiritual need for peace within the context of an experience of relaxation. Peace and relaxation belong together in the minds of most people. When under heavy stress, we often say, "I need a little peace and relaxation." What are we looking for? Certainly relief from stress. But more than that, we're looking for renewal and restoration, for a closer connection to ourselves, to others, to the world, and to God. When we're under heavy pressure, it's hard even to be aware of this need, much less act on it. That's why relaxation is so valuable. It reduces the stress and thus provides the space for a more open awareness of the spiritual need for peace, for wholeness.

People meet their need for peace and relaxation in many different ways. Most of them are nonreligious: vacations, getting away for a weekend, making room for "down time" in one's schedule, spending quiet time with a friend, taking a hike in the woods—thousands of different ways. The purpose of this exercise is to put peace and relaxation into the context of one's relationship to God, reminding ourselves that the source of our wholeness is in God and that our renewal and restoration in every realm is ultimately dependent on our relationship to God. Thus the title of the exercise: "Relaxing into the Peace of God."

Since this exercise was designed for use in stressful situations, the relaxation instructions at the beginning are longer than usual. If you use this exercise with persons experiencing acute stress, it will be useful to follow the exercise with a discussion of strategies for self-care in times of stress.

Guided Imagery

We'll begin with a method of relaxation that tenses and then relaxes the muscles in different portions of your body. Tense the muscles in your face, hold them in tension until the count of five, and then let them completely relax . . . . . Tense the muscles in the region of your neck and shoulders, hold them in tension until the count of five, and then let them completely relax . . . . . Tense the muscles in your hands and arms by clenching your fists and bending your arms at the elbows as tightly as you can, hold them in tension until the count of five, and then let them completely relax . . . . . Tense the muscles in your chest and abdomen by holding your breath and tightening the muscles around your stomach, hold them in tension until the count of five, and then let them completely relax . . . . . Tense the muscles in your thighs, legs, and feet, hold them in tension until the count of five, and then let them completely relax.

Letting the weight of your body be fully supported by the chair on which you are sitting or the bed or floor on which you are lying, close your eyes or keep them focused on one place in the room so that you will not be distracted by anything outside the world of your inner experience . . . feeling more and more relaxed as you move deeper into the world of your inner experience . . . freed from all outside distractions, with nothing more important for you to do . . . paying attention only to your breathing, the natural rhythm of your body . . . breathing in . . . and breathing out . . . breathing in the air of life . . . and breathing out all worry and tension . . . feeling yourself becoming more and more relaxed . . . letting any distracting thoughts fade out of consciousness without any effort on your part . . .

relaxing into the arms of God and trusting the strong but gentle holding you find there . . . letting your breathing come more slowly and evenly, each breath bringing a deeper sense of relaxation. (*Pause for 30 seconds*)

Let your mind drift back over the years and recall moments, perhaps even prolonged periods, of utter relaxation and feelings of calm and peacefulness. It may have been just a brief interlude during a time of considerable stress and tension, or it may have been a period of prolonged restfulness in your life. I'll give you time to recall four or five such times in the last few years. Don't feel rushed. Take the time to savor the goodness of those special moments in your life. (*Pause for 2 minutes*)

Select one of the occasions that you have recalled in order to enter more deeply into the experience. Choose one where you felt a strong sense of connectedness, where you readily and easily felt peaceful. If you are not immediately aware of which experience you would like to return to with the aid of your imagination, take the time to recall each one again. (*Pause for 30 seconds*)

In your mind's eye, reenter that experience of profound peace and relaxation. Within the world of your inner experience you can do that with great vividness, as if you were experiencing it all over again. Let the scene unfold in your mind so that your inner eye can see all that you saw then. Listen for the sounds that you heard then. Feel the touch of things within your reach, including the experience of being touched if that is part of your memory of this occasion. Be aware as well of any smells that are associated with that time and place, perhaps of someone you love. As you enter more deeply into that experience of rest and relaxation with all of your senses, feel the peace and goodness that you felt then. (*Pause for 30 seconds*)

If there were others with you, recall the difference that their presence made on your peace of mind. Listen again to what is being said, and notice its effect on you. Maybe it's nothing that is said but just the presence of this person or persons that fills you with a sense of wholeness and goodness. Or perhaps no one else is there, and it's the solitude that is good, the feeling of being at peace with yourself, an inner harmony of body, mind, and spirit. Whether alone or with others, let the experience deepen until the present merges with the past and you are fully inside this experience of deep relaxation. (*Pause for 1 minute*)

Do you sense the peace of God in this place? Where is God in this experience? Deep inside you? In the natural surroundings? In the presence of another? Concentrate your attention on the peace of God for the next few moments. Find a word or a phrase that will heighten your awareness of God's peace. It can be anything, from the Latin phrase *dona nobis pacem* (grant us peace) to simply the word *peace* or *peace of God*. Say the word or phrase each time you exhale, letting the peace of God fill your soul with its goodness. (*Pause for 2 minutes*)

Staying within this state of profound relaxation and peace, call to mind something that brings tension and stress into your life at this time. It can be anything: something you have to do, a troubled relationship, a decision you have to make. (*Pause for 20 seconds*) While still within the experience of peaceful relaxation, picture yourself responding to that stressful situation. With tender care, gently guide the you who is tense and stressful into the relaxed and peaceful world that you have been experiencing. Feel the lines on your face and the muscles of your body relaxing as the tension slowly drains from your body like rainwater flowing gently down the side of a hill. Surround yourself in whatever stressful situation you're in with the peacefulness that comes from God, from others, from nature, from deep within yourself. The peace that you are experiencing now is the wholeness that God intends for you. Let yourself relax into the peace of God as the tension gradually eases and you feel more and more restored to wholeness. (*Pause for 1 minute*)

Gradually reorient yourself to this room, refreshed in body, mind, and spirit, and confident that the peace of God, both from within you and from beyond you, will continue to bring calm and peacefulness to whatever situation of stress you might face.

Gratitude

Introduction

Gratitude and praise are our most natural and spontaneous responses to awareness of the grace and goodness of God in our lives. Psalms 103 and 104 are good examples of this. We're most likely to give thanks in periods of relative wellness, especially after or during recovery. Being aware of gratitude is more difficult during times of quiet desperation and great neediness.

Why, then, is this exercise placed in a chapter on meeting spiritual needs? There are two reasons. First, we rarely think of gratitude as a spiritual need, though we are quick to say thank you for the smallest of favors. The need for giving and receiving thanks is regularly met on the horizontal plane, even if only in perfunctory ways; it is on the vertical plane that we are most likely to be aware of our need for blessing and for grateful hearts with which to receive it. The church's liturgy and the Christian's prayer life are the primary structures within which this spiritual need can be met. This exercise can be used within either of those structures.

A second reason that this exercise belongs in a chapter on meeting spiritual needs is because that need is often felt most poignantly after recovery from illness or some other personal crisis, especially if the event evokes a sense of wonder, such as the birth of a child. At such times one can and should be grateful to nurses, physicians, and anyone else who has provided physical, psychological, or spiritual care. But the overwhelming need is for giving thanks to God, whose providential care has been experienced in the care of others and yet extends infinitely beyond it.

This exercise can be used for different purposes. The first part of the exercise is well suited for groups and general occasions, such as a portion of a homily at a service of thanksgiving. The second part is designed primarily for private use and for the spiritual care of people whose hearts are full of gratitude for their recovery from illness, from some form of addiction, or from some other personal crisis. The two parts will work well as one unit for some purposes, such as use by a recovery group.

Guided Imagery

Take a deep breath and exhale, letting all of the air out of your lungs. Do that again, noticing how your body naturally becomes more relaxed as you exhale. Once again take a deep breath and exhale, this time imagining all the tension and worry of your life flowing out of your body as you exhale.

Letting your breathing become more steady and relaxed, attune yourself to its natural rhythm . . . breathing in . . . and breathing out . . . the natural rhythm of your breathing from the time you were born until the time you die . . . breathing in the breath of life . . . breathing out all tension and worry. As you continue to focus your attention on your breathing, say the words "Praise God" with each breath that you exhale, continuing with that breath prayer until I tell you to stop. (*Pause for 1–2 minutes*)

With the aid of your imagination, go to a sanctuary in nature that you love and treasure, a sanctuary because it is a holy place for you, a place where you feel the presence of God in a particularly strong way. Though others may know of this place, imagine that you are alone. Very gradually look around you . . . feasting your eyes on the beauty of this place . . . pausing to wonder at the intricacies of design in all that you see . . . noticing the perfect blend of colors, unmatched by any human creation. Listen for the sounds in this place . . . the chirping of birds, the flowing of water or the pounding of waves, the whistling of wind through the trees, or perhaps just the sound of silence. Touch and smell the flowers, if there are any there. As your experience of the goodness of this place deepens within you, imagine how you might express your gratitude to God for being there. Maybe through music: by singing or playing an instrument or directing an orchestra. Or maybe by building an altar for worshiping God. Follow the lead of your imagination in any way it takes you as you express your thanksgiving for the goodness of creation. (*Pause for 1 minute*)

Turn your attention from the wonders of creation in nature to the wonders of creation in yourself. Imagine that you have a vantage point from within yourself where you can observe the intricacies of your vision, which adjusts automatically for light and distance, instantly transmitting the constant flow of images that are received to the brain for processing or storage. (*Pause for 20 seconds*) Imagine that you have a similar vantage point to observe your hearing, which discerns a wide variety of sound waves, communicating them to the brain and coordinating them with visual images. (*Pause for 20 seconds*) Imagine that you can see from within the working of your heart, the flow of blood throughout your body, and the activity of cells within your immune system warding off disease. (*Pause for 30 seconds*) As your appreciation deepens for the complexity of your body's functioning, imagine how you might express your gratitude to God for the wonder of this creation. Maybe through song or prayer or some other form of praise. Or your imagination may suggest something that will be a surprise even to you. (*Pause for 1 minute*)

With the aid of your memory and your imagination, re-enter the experience of your recent adversity from its beginning to its successful resolution. Recall the onset of this period of crisis. How sudden was it? And how surprised were you? Are you aware of negative feelings like anger and depression as the full impact of this adversity hits home? How well do you cope with negative feelings? Do you remember turning to God? Or did God seem distant and unavailable? (*Pause for 30 seconds*)

Letting the story of this adversity unfold naturally within your awareness to the point of its most critical juncture, recall the feelings and thoughts you had about yourself, about your loved ones, about God. Are you aware of any significant changes taking place in you? (*Pause for 30 seconds*)

With the aid of your memory and imagination, reenter the experience of recovery from this adversity. When were you first aware of a change? Was the change sudden and dramatic or rather a subtle shift within yourself that you were aware of only by hindsight? Feel again what you were feeling then. Were there feelings of relief? of liberation?

of joy? of hope? of gratitude? . . . Focus on the feelings of gratitude for the help that others gave, and express that in any way that seems appropriate. (*Pause for 30 seconds*)

Where is God in the experience of your recovery? Do you experience God as strong deliverer? as healer? as sustainer and supporter? Express your gratitude to God for your recovery in any way that seem appropriate to you. (*Pause for 1 minute*)

Acceptance

The need for acceptance is closely related to the need for forgiveness and love, two other prominent spiritual needs. The difference between acceptance and love is that acceptance implies some kind of impediment that love must overcome. One might call it an "in spite of" kind of love. Both forgiveness and acceptance imply this "in spite of" kind of love, but acceptance is a much broader term. You need to be accepted not only when you've wronged someone but also when your body is disfigured and/or foul-smelling as a result of illness or when you feel inadequate after failing an exam or losing a job.

We never fully meet our expectations of ourselves. We all experience deficits in one form or another, deficits in appearance, performance, attitude, and other measurements of our worth. That's why acceptance is a universal human need. The fear is that we will be rejected if we don't measure up to the ideal self that is the standard by which we judge ourselves and expect to be judged by others and God. This is the tyranny of living under the law and its harsh demands. There is no way that we will ever succeed in assuring ourselves that we are completely acceptable.

I do not want to suggest, however, that acceptance is a spiritual need only because of sin. It would be a universal human need in a perfect creation. Our lack of perfection is due as much to finitude as to sin. Our wholeness is always in the process of becoming as we develop into the persons God intends us to be. That developmental journey leads through such precarious periods as adolescence, midlife crisis, and the physical deterioration of aging, each of which generates a need for acceptance in those who face the adversities such periods bring.

This exercise can be used in a variety of settings: as a wellness exercise in almost any group, for a person who is feeling unloved and unacceptable for some particular reason, and for self-care. The private use of this exercise has the additional advantage of reinforcing acceptance of oneself.

Guided Imagery

Be as comfortable as you can in the position you're in . . . relaxing your body until it feels as limp and free of tension as when you are asleep . . . letting all distracting thoughts float aimlessly by without heeding them . . . attending only to the stillness of this quiet sanctuary and the solitude it provides for your journey inward to the center of your self . . . breathing evenly and slowly . . . moving deeper and deeper into the regions of your inner self . . . conscious only of the peace and tranquillity of being in the quiet sanctuary that has been created for you in this place and during this time . . . no one making demands on your time or expecting anything at all from you . . . free to be yourself without anyone peering over your shoulder or passing judgment on what you think or feel . . . breathing evenly and slowly . . . paying attention only to your breathing . . . becoming still and calm within the peace of the inner world of your being.

In your mind's eye, imagine yourself as an infant in your mother's arms or the arms of anyone you wish. Imagine that you are in a church at a worship service or in some other public place if that feels safer or more natural. Within the safety of the quiet sanctuary of your inner world, give yourself permission to feel as vulnerable as a helpless and dependent infant. Feel the goodness and the safety of arms completely encircling you and holding you firmly but gently. (*Pause for 15 seconds*)

Within this warm and gentle holding, imagine yourself becoming very needy. Perhaps you are feeling strong hunger pangs, or wet diapers are making you uncomfortable, or something has frightened you. Picture yourself crying, only whimpering at first, but as the neediness increases, crying harder and harder, your tiny body thrashing about as you become more and more distressed. Imagine some of the people sitting around you giving disapproving glances to you and the person holding you because of the noise and general disturbance you are causing. (*Pause for 15 seconds*)

Experience now the warm response and gentle care given by the person holding you. Imagine that she or he gets up and, with no sign of irritation, carries you away from the crowd of people who are impatient with you. Taking your frantic crying with utter seriousness, imagine the person searching for the cause of your distress. Feel the goodness of the care you receive as you are fed or changed or soothed by soft cooing and gentle rocking. Feel the goodness of being totally accepted as the helpless and dependent infant you are—with all of your neediness, irritability, and screaming impatience. (*Pause for 30 seconds*)

With the aid of your memory, retrace the steps of your journey through life and recall experiences of being completely accepted by another person or by God. Rather than just remembering the event, enter into the felt sense of the experience of being accepted. Go back as far as you can remember, trusting your intuition and your feeling response to help you identify the most significant experiences of being accepted. Choose four or five such experiences and jot down a word or phrase that will identify the experience. (*Pause for 1 minute*)

Choose one of the experiences that you selected, the one that evokes the strongest sense of being fully accepted without any reservations. (*Pause for 15 seconds*) With the aid of your memory and your imagination, reenter that experience of being fully accepted. Picture the setting in your mind: the time, the place, the circumstances that led up to the occasion. Feel the neediness that you were feeling then. What was it that was making you feel unsure about yourself and your world at that time? Is it safe for you to be as needy as you feel right now? Or is there an inner voice telling you to be strong, to be grown up, to hide your feelings and handle it all by yourself? (*Pause for 10 seconds*)

Picture the person who accepts you so totally. What does she or he do or say? (*Pause for 15 seconds*) How do you respond? (*Pause for 15 seconds*) Enter as fully as you can into that experience of being accepted without reservation. (*Pause for 15 seconds*) Where is God, if anywhere, in this experience? Is it God's acceptance that you are experiencing, perhaps through the acceptance of another person? How is this experience of being accepted similar to or different from the experience of being accepted by Christ? Immerse yourself deeply in the experience of being accepted, whatever the source of that acceptance may be. (*Pause for 1 minute*)

From within the safe world of your inner experience, pay attention to your neediness right now. Are you aware of feelings of being unloved and not accepted by yourself? by others? by God? Is illness the reason? self-esteem? behavior that has been hurtful? perceived inadequacies on your part? Take a moment to deepen your experience of needing acceptance—without any attempt on your part to lessen that need or explain it away. (*Pause for 30 seconds*)

Imagine the healing presence of Christ at your side. Express to him in any way that seems appropriate what you have been experiencing. Let him see how needy you are, trusting that he will respond to your neediness with acceptance and love. (*Pause for 30 seconds*) Let your imagination suggest a way in which Jesus shows you his total acceptance and unconditional love through what he says or does. Simply let that happen without trying to direct it or make it come out in some particular way, trusting your imagination to lead you through that experience in a way that is appropriate. (*Pause for 2 minutes*)

As you feel ready, come away from this experience of profound acceptance, knowing that nothing you can imagine, not even your death, can separate you from the love of Christ. Imagine the healing presence of Christ still with you as you reorient yourself to this room, ready to resume your journey through life.

Chapter 4

Wellness Exercises

Historically both the church and medicine have paid much more attention to healing than to the prevention of illness through promoting wellness. That is changing now as a result of a growing interest in health maintenance, an interest that sometimes, however, borders on preoccupation. When that happens, health can become a form of idolatry, the organizing center of one's life. Preoccupation with health can also be a not-so-subtle form of death denial, as if one could by the right habits subvert or control the power of death. A sweatshirt that I saw on a jogger put it in proper perspective: "Eat well! Exercise regularly! Die anyway!"

Although wellness is never an end in itself, it is what God intends for us within the larger context of our mission as God's people, a mission of service to God and humanity. Our model is Christ, "this man for others." Nothing in Jesus' time even comes close to the current wellness movement, but there was encouragement to enjoy and use to their fullest the wonderful gifts of life and health that come from God.

The exercises in this chapter use the imagery of faith to facilitate wholeness of body, mind, and spirit. There are exercises to aid relaxation, reduce anxiety, make transitions, enhance communal wellness, and experience the freedom of Christ. In each case no deficit is assumed in the person doing the exercise, only the desire to attain the fullness of being that God intends for each of us.

Communal Wellness

I COR. 12:4-27

Introduction

Saint Paul uses the metaphor of the human body to describe the church in this familiar passage from 1 Corinthians. The strength of Paul's image of the church as the body of Christ is that it is so concrete, so easy to visualize. We constantly interact with embodied persons and know ourselves only as embodied persons. And we all know what it's like to have sores on our body or a virus that threatens the carefully balanced harmony of the body or a general listlessness that comes from who knows where. And we all know what it's like to feel well, full of energy that enables us to lean into life, eager to meet whatever opportunities and challenges await us. Such experiences provide us with rich resources for a guided imagery exercise on communal wellness.

The purpose of the exercise is to celebrate the health of the church, discern the illnesses that threaten it, participate in the spiritual healing that can restore its wholeness, and be energized for the mission of being a healing church. The exercise can be done as a prayer of the church, as a meditation on 1 Corinthians 12 within a Bible study group, or as a homily within a liturgy that gives communal expression to what it means to be the church. The exercises can also be used to focus the experience of being the church within a family or any other group that shares a common faith in Christ. The exercise is likely to work best in a small group because of the opportunity to share the experience later. However, larger assemblies, such as a worship service for five hundred, have an even greater need for such an exercise. The experience of the church as the body of Christ is often most lacking there, and an exercise that fosters a sense of communal wholeness can be valuable.

Those doing the exercise should be told in advance that they will be asked to grasp the hand of the person on either side of them during the exercise. Make sure that everybody is within the reach of at least one other person.

Situate your body as comfortably as you can in the chair where you are sitting, letting the chair bear the weight of your body, as the ground beneath bears the weight of the chair, supporting you as it supports everything that rests on it. As you relax, you will feel the tension drain out of your muscles . . . muscles on your forehead, face, and jaw, becoming limp as the tension drains away . . . muscles in your shoulders and neck becoming as limp as a balloon with all the air drained out . . . muscles in your upper arms, forearms, and fingers, at rest and free of all tension . . . muscles in your chest and abdomen becoming more and more relaxed and at rest . . . muscles in your thighs, calves, and feet, feeling as limp and relaxed as a rag doll lying on the sofa.

Let yourself drift ever so gently toward the center of your inner being . . . attuning yourself to the world within rather than the world without . . . becoming aware of your body from within, your body that is you, your breathing a natural and regular rhythm of your body . . . letting your body become more and more relaxed . . . finding peace and contentment from within the center of yourself. (*Pause for 20 seconds*)

In your mind's eye, imagine that you are able to see what is going on inside your body. From a vantage point within your body, imagine that you are able to observe the wonders of your vision, how it works, how your mind comes to recognize what you see and fit it in with the rest of what you know. It's not important that you've got it right anatomically but that you gain a sense of wonder and awe at the complexity and perfection of the process. (*Pause for 20 seconds*) Now imagine that you are able to observe the wonders of your hearing — its complexity and perfection (*Pause for 20 seconds*). Now imagine that you can observe the operation of all the muscles from within your body, the grace and ease with which they move in response to command in a symphony of motion. (*Pause for 20 seconds*) Pay particular attention to the unity of all the diverse and complex functions of your body, each part complementing and supporting the other parts. (*Pause for 30 seconds*)

Still attentive to the wonder of the harmonious unity within your body, reach out to the persons on either side of you and grasp the hand that is reaching out to you. (*Pause for 10 seconds*) As you do so, feel the energy coming to you from both sides and connecting you to every other person who is here. (*Pause for 20 seconds*) Picture a flow of energy or light linking you to every other person in this room and forming one harmonious body. Experience that flow of energy as the Spirit of God binding us all together as one body in Christ. Sense the presence of Christ within you and between you and every other person in this room. (*Pause for 30 seconds*)

Release the hands on either side of you, keeping your attention focused on the experience of being linked together as one body in Christ. (*Pause for 10 seconds*) Let pictures of people who contribute to the health of this congregational community form within your mind's eye. As each picture comes into the field of your inner vision, let a circle of light surround the image as a halo, and feel the goodness of this person as a gift of the Spirit to this community, a gift that makes for wellness in the body of Christ. You may be surprised at some of the persons you become conscious of. Don't second-guess your intuitions. Simply surround the person with a circle of light and sense the goodness of the gift this person brings to communal wellness. Take a few minutes to celebrate the gifts of the Spirit to this community. (*Pause for 2 minutes*)

If the church is the body of Christ, and if that body is sometimes ailing, then what are the sores that keep your church from being a healthy and harmonious body of Christ? Are you aware of listlessness, a lack of energy within the body? Is there tension existing between persons or between different factions within the community? Has the tension in some cases hardened into conflict? As you become aware of any weakness or illness that afflicts the body of Christ of which you are a part and thus afflicts you, pray for healing, not just for individuals, though that's where the symptoms may appear, but for the whole body of Christ that it may be healed. Take a moment to focus your consciousness on the community as ill and in need of healing. (*Pause for 2 minutes*)

Imagine the Spirit of God as a healing presence within this community, moving in and through the members of the community, strengthening bonds where they are weak, reconciling those who are in tension and conflict, energizing the body where there is apathy, and bringing unity and harmony to the whole body. (*Pause for 30 seconds*) Imagine yourself as a vital organ in a communal organism that is healed, revitalized, unified, and purposeful. What signs would you look for as evidence of healing? What would count as evidence of wellness? (*Pause for 1 minute*)

Focus your attention on where you see yourself within the body of Christ. Finish this sentence: "Within the body of Christ I can best be a . . . " Would that be an ear? a tongue? hands or feet? What are the ways in which you contribute to both the illness and the wellness of the body of Christ? Take a moment to reflect on the joys and tribulations of being the body of Christ in this place and how you can be a better source of blessing and healing within this community. (*Pause for 1–2 minutes*)

Why Worry?

MATTHEW 6:25-34

Introduction

Worry is the imagination gone sour, focusing on negative rather than positive outcomes. We worry when we face demands that seem overwhelming and deadlines that loom over us like death threats. We see storm clouds on the horizon, if not directly overhead, in the form of mounting bills, poor health, job-related problems, family issues. Sometimes we are not aware of just how high the anxiety level has become until it stands in sharp contrast with the relief that we feel on weekends or when we take a vacation. Many people have an inner sense that they are always living on the edge, fearing that some event will push them over the edge and out of control.

What is more, clinical evidence shows that our physical health can suffer from the effects of anxiety. Studies reveal that the increasing stress of living in the modern era can depress the function of the immune system in some people and can contribute to the risk of heart disease. The danger of stress-related illness is highest, according to these studies, when feelings of depression, loss of control, and helplessness and hopelessness are present.

In the Sermon on the Mount, Jesus speaks directly to the anxiety that inevitably accompanies the awareness of our vulnerability. Though not sin, anxiety is fertile ground for the temptation to sin. Anxiety is the awareness of our finitude, the realization that we are creatures and not God, that there are limits to how much control we exercise in our lives. The answer to anxiety is faith, without which we cannot live. The temptation is to put faith in something that is less than God, something that seems powerful but is slated for destruction along with the rest of the created order. Anything that promises security in times of high stress and personal vulnerability is a likely candidate for idolatry, whether another person, financial security, good health, or countless other objects of misplaced faith.

The only sure foundation of true faith, as Jesus reminds us in this portion of the Sermon on the Mount, is to be found in the promises of God. So why worry? That is the theme of this Scripture passage and the imagery exercise based on it. God is in control, even when the limits of our own control are so blatantly obvious. Anxiety, the universal human condition, is the precursor of both sin and faith. The purpose of this exercise is to strengthen the response of faith and keep it deeply rooted in the promises of God.

Though this passage of Scripture will probably be familiar to most of the participants in the exercise, it should be read in advance and commented on briefly. The NRSV is used in the exercise. If you introduce the exercise by reading from another version, make the necessary adjustments in the exercise.

Guided Imagery

As the quietness deepens within you, let your eyes close or keep them focused on one place in the room to avoid outside distraction and to focus more clearly on your inner experience. Imagine that you are in a lovely meadow in the springtime, a meadow full of wildflowers that seem to be dancing in the warm and gentle breezes. Feel the warmth of the sun, and catch the scent of the flowers in the air. Imagine your favorite birds flying above you, lazily gliding through the sky with wings outstretched, carefree. With the aid of your imagination, find a comfortable place in the luxurious grass of the meadow and feel your body relax as you let go of the tensions and worries that have been close to the surface of your consciousness . . . letting them fly away like birds that have been freed from a cage . . . becoming aware of how much more relaxed and peaceful you feel in this meadow than you have felt for a long time . . . letting your breathing come more slowly and evenly . . . letting the inner stillness wrap itself around your soul . . . feeling your worries and tensions flowing out of you as you exhale, and feeling the Spirit of God filling you each time you inhale . . . tensions flowing out . . . the Spirit of God flowing in . . . beathing in . . . and breathing out . . . with each breath becoming more and more relaxed, more and more in tune with the slow and graceful rhythm of nature that surrounds you in the meadow.

Jesus says: "Look at the birds of the air; they neither sow nor reap nor gather into barns, and yet your heavenly Father feeds them. Are you not of more value than they? . . . Consider the lilies of the field, how they grow; they neither toil nor spin; yet I tell you, even Solomon in all his glory was not clothed like one of these."

In your mind's eye, picture one of the wildflowers that grow so luxuriantly in the meadow all around you. Any flower will do. Look at this flower very carefully and notice the colors . . . the fragrance . . . the texture . . . the intricacy of the design of the flower, each part in perfect proportion with every other part. Look closely at the delicate colors, brighter and more evenly matched than anything in human creation. See the flower as a growing plant. In your mind's eye, see it drawing water and nutrients from the soil and life-giving energy from the sun. Take a moment to reflect on the wonder of growing things, seeing in this flower the beauty and majesty of the whole creation . . .

Imagine yourself as being like that flower, growing naturally and without effort, rooted in your family, your church, your network of friends, and at the same time reaching out beyond yourself as you are drawn by the light of Christ. Take a moment to reflect on the goodness of being rooted in communities that sustain you and of being drawn toward self-transcendence by the light of God's grace and power, and all without any effort or worry on your part. (*Pause for 1 minute*)

Now imagine that you are watching time-lapse pictures of your own human development, slowly unfolding from a fertilized egg to the mature person you are today. Picture yourself as an embryo inside your mother's womb, secure in that environment, and slowly and effortlessly forming organs and other tissues until the infant body is fully formed. Picture yourself as you were born, and then at five-year intervals until the present, gradually becoming the person you are. Note the effortless ease of the process: no frantic striving, no anxiety, no toil, but rather a free flow of graceful movement from one stage to the next. Sense the wonder and goodness of creation, flowing freely out of the bounty of God. The deeper you penetrate into the mystery of the neverending flow of life, the deeper your trust in God, who is the source of all that is or ever will be. Take a moment to let the experience deepen, the experience of created goodness, flowing freely out of the bounty of God. (*Pause for 1 minute*)

Turning from the past to the future, consider for a moment what lies ahead of you in different spheres of your life: school, home, office, friends, projects, whatever comes to your mind. As you do so, be sensitive to anxious feelings that are generated when you anticipate some event or decision that lies ahead of you. As you become aware of rising anxiety, jot down a word or phrase on your paper that will remind you of what prompted your anxiety. Then let your thoughts turn to something else about the future that makes you anxious until you have noted four or five different events or challenges that generate some anxiety within you. (*Pause for 1 minute*)

Opening your eyes just long enough to scan the list of items, choose one of them that you would like to reflect on more deeply. It can be any one of them, not necessarily the one that causes the most anxiety. (*Pause for 20 seconds*) What about this event or decision makes you anxious? Is it fear that you won't be up to the challenge? Is it dealing with someone who makes you uncomfortable, or doing something unpleasant? Be as honest with yourself as you can about what worries you. (*Pause for 1 minute*)

In your mind's eye, imagine that future event or decision unfolding, not as you fear it might but according to the providence of God, who cares for you much more than for the birds of the air and flowers of the field. Imagine yourself moving into whatever the future holds with a deep inner awareness of the presence and power of God. (*Pause for 20 seconds*) What is the best thing that you can imagine happening? What would God wish for you in this situation? Imagine God as being in the future and beckoning you forward. You may hear a voice calling you or see a figure waiting for you or urging you forward, or you may just sense a presence ahead of you making it safe to move forward with confidence that you will not be alone, no matter what the future holds. As that experience deepens, begin to write about the difference it makes when you face the future with trust and hope rather than with worry and fear. (*Allow 10–15 minutes for writing*)

Relaxing into the Love of God

Prayer begins with relaxation and an awareness of the presence of God. Only rarely do people begin their prayers by self-consciously relaxing and concentrating on the presence of God, but the times and places set aside for prayer condition us for both. Prayer at the end of the day coincides with the natural rhythm of relaxation that comes in the transition period between activity and sleep. Conditions that we regard as important for prayer (quieting of both body and mind, eliminating external noises and distractions) are also necessary conditions for relaxation. We also do things to heighten our awareness of God's presence when we pray. Choices we make about the place of prayer, such as church, and the posture of prayer, such as kneeling with head bowed, heighten our awareness of the presence of God.

If we do, in fact, prepare ourselves for prayer in the ways just suggested, then we can strengthen our prayer life by learning ways to facilitate relaxation and an awareness of the presence of God. Guided imagery is a wonderful tool for both. Though people quite naturally relax as they pray, guided imagery can deepen that relaxation. This is why each imagery exercise begins with relaxation techniques. The advantage of that, as has been suggested throughout this guidebook, is that relaxation facilitates a movement from primarily verbal, linear thought patterns to brain activity that is more holistic and imaginative. Though we can pray by using both words and images, images are more likely to evoke the experience of God's presence. A crucifix, a vaulted ceiling, an organ prelude, and the smell of incense are more likely to awaken the sense of God's presence than abstract doctrinal propositions. Most of us are aware of this when we reflect on our most profound prayer experiences, but we don't often self-consciously nurture such experience. Imagery is a tool for entering deeply into a prayer state.

The following exercise is devoted to facilitating relaxation and an awareness of God's presence. That alone qualifies it as an exercise for both healing and wellness, though I regard these as by-products of this form of prayer rather than its chief purpose. The chief purpose for this and all prayer is the worship of God, whose love is the source of our life and the hope of our future.

Guided Imagery

Focus your awareness on your body, paying attention to places where you feel tension—perhaps in your shoulders or the back of your neck, perhaps in your lower back or in the pit of your stomach. Wherever you are feeling tension, stretch the muscles in that region and then let them relax. (*Pause for 30 seconds*) Feel the tension drain away as you relax, like air being released from a balloon. Rotate your shoulders by bringing them up and then forward . . . and then up and to the back . . . feeling the tension drain away as you do so. Rotate your neck around on its axis . . . first one way . . . then the other . . . feeling the tension drain away as you do so.

Sitting in quiet and calm . . . letting your body become heavy and your spirit light . . . letting your eyes gently close and your breathing come evenly and slowly. As the stillness deepens, let your mind slow its pace, adjusting its rhythm to the tempo of your breathing . . . breathing in . . . and breathing out . . . body and mind becoming quieter with the steady rhythm of your breathing . . . bringing stillness and peace to your inner being . . . letting the concerns and problems of the day float away like balloons carried aloft by gentle winds . . . hearing the sounds of silence . . . feeling the soft beauty of the inner world that beckons you deeper and deeper into the center of your being.

Centered within your inner being, conscious only of your breath moving . . . moving in . . . and moving out of the center of your being . . . letting the quiet deepen within the center of yourself . . . feeling God's Spirit moving within you . . . waiting calmly for the awareness of God's presence to grow and fill the depths of your inner spirit. (*Pause for 1 minute*)

With the aid of your imagination, picture a broad mountain meadow surrounded by tall snow-covered peaks. In the meadow is a large lake filled with deep blue water fed by mountain streams, one of which is flowing into the lake near where you are standing. Though the sun is bright on this warm summer day, the gentle breeze feels cool in the high mountain air. Feel the breeze on your face and arms and notice how it softly sways the tops of the pine trees. Listen to the lapping of the waves against the shoreline. Breathe in the fresh, clean, clear air of this mountain paradise, each breath filling you with new energy and peace. (*Pause for 30 seconds*)

Imagine that you are walking along the shore of this lake. It is late in the afternoon, and the sun is moving toward the horizon. The sun is a golden blazing yellow and the sky a brilliant blue. The water of the lake mirrors the snow-capped mountains. Hear the call of familiar birds in the woods nearby and the sound of a fish breaking the surface in the lake. Let the beauty of the surroundings fill your soul with a deep sense of peace and contentment. (*Pause for 1 minute*)

As you walk along the shore, you come to a mound covered with summer flowers of many different colors. Find a place to sit in the luxurious grass on the crest of the mound and look out over the lake. Transfixed by the beauty of the scene, you gaze intently at the light of the sun reflected in the deep-blue water of the lake. (*Pause for 30 seconds*)

Feel the presence of God in this place: in the sunlight on the water, in the sounds of lake and forest, in the air you are breathing, in the mystery of nature's beauty . . . knowing you can see more deeply into things than before . . . that you can hear more than your ear could ever discern . . . that you can know the truth at the core of your being as you never did before. Resting quietly in the center of yourself, you are aware of the presence of the Spirit of God within you and around you—in all that there is. (*Pause for 30 seconds*)

With the summer flowers of many colors all around you, the words of the psalmist come to mind: "As for mortals, their days are like grass; they flourish like a flower of the field; for the wind passes over it, and it is gone, and its place knows it no more." Take moment to reflect on the goodness of life and its swift passage. (*Pause for 1 minute*)

"But the steadfast love of the Lord is from everlasting to everlasting on those who fear him, . . . to those who keep his covenant." A love that is forever. Imagine the love of God surrounding you like a blanket . . . letting yourself sink deeply into that love, knowing that it will never end . . . . . Take a moment to reflect on the difference between this moment of inner peace and joy which will fade and the steadfast love of God which is forever. (*Pause for 1 minute*)

Relaxing into the love of God, let your breathing become an inner prayer. As you exhale say within yourself, "Bless the Lord, O my soul." With your next breath do the same; as you exhale, say within yourself, "Bless the Lord, O my soul." Continue with that breath prayer of blessing until I tell you to stop, feeling yourself surrounded by God's love . . . imagining yourself nestled safely in a blanket, held within the powerful but gentle hands of God. (*Pause for 2 minutes*)

As you feel ready, gently bring yourself back to this room and the company of others who share your faith and hope, refreshed in body and soul by your experience of deep relaxation and awareness of the presence of God, and knowing you can return to this place anytime that you wish to renew your sense of peace and purpose.

Imaging the Image of God

Introduction

"God created humankind in his image, in the image of God he created them; male and female he created them" (Gen. 1:27). Realizing the created goodness of the "image of God" is the key to spiritual wellness as Christians understand it. Though the phrase is not defined in Scripture, the general meaning is clear enough. God wants us to be like God without acting as if we were God, a distinction that people have had difficulty with since the beginning of the race. There are all sorts of clues throughout Scripture that tell us what it's like to be in the image of God. The best clues, of course, come from Jesus, who is the incarnate image of God on earth. We are fortunate to have such a concrete image of God to guide us. Models are much better guides than definitions when we're trying to grasp what it means to be like God. We also know people who model for us the image cf God, and the models are infinitely varied in color of skin, ethnic origin, personality characteristics, social role, and life-style.

For all of these reasons, "imaging the image of God" is a useful exercise for spiritual wellness. We can imagine the kind of people that God would have us be with full confidence that we will not be misled, as we may be in wellness exercises designed for nothing more than personal self-gratification and enhancement. There are many different ways that the image of God can be expressed in the lives of Christians. One of the wonders of creation is the absolute uniqueness of every human person, and thus the absolute uniqueness of the image of God that each person can realize within himself or herself. Though many people may choose a similar model for what it means to be in the image of God, such as Mother Teresa, the way in which that image is given concrete expression will be unique to each person's experience and potential.

Find a position in the chair where you are sitting that feels comfortable, keeping your feet flat on the floor and your back straight. Close your eyes or keep them focused on one place in the room in order to avoid distraction from the outside world, a world that demands your attention almost every waking hour . . . paying attention instead to your breathing . . . attuning yourself to its natural rhythm . . . letting your breathing come more slowly and evenly. As you breathe in, imagine the Spirit of God coming into you . . . filling your lungs with spiritual energy . . . breathing in the breath of God that first filled Adam's lungs . . . and breathing out impurities and fears and negative feelings . . . breathing in the breath of God that sustains you every moment of your life . . . and breathing out everything that keeps you from being the image of God . . . feeling your whole body pulsing with the life-giving energy of the Spirit of God . . . every breath the breath of God, every breath the Spirit of God filling your spirit with energy and power . . . breathing in the breath of God . . . breathing out fear and anxiety . . . breathing in the Spirit of God . . . breathing out all that keeps you from being the image of God.

Let your imagination suggest to you what the image of God might look like . . . or sound like . . . or feel like. Let images surface spontaneously in your mind without any effort on your part to censor or prejudge what they should be. It may be an image of a person who embodies for you what God is like or some quality of an animal such as strength or gentleness, or something in nature that suggests the image of God to you, such as the majesty of a mountain. Or you may hear music that suggests God for you. Trust your intuitions. As images or sounds or actions come to mind, jot down a word or phrase that captures the felt sense of God. (*Pause for 2 minutes*)

Returning to the world of your inner experience, go back to the day of your baptism with the aid of your imaginating, even if you were only an infant. Reconstruct the place, the time, and the people who were there. Experience the feeling of solidarity with those who are there, and check to see if you have any intimations of the larger company of saints that surround those who are surrounding you. Feel the gentle touch of a hand making the sign of the cross on your forehead. Picture the water flowing over you and hear the words being said as that happens, "I baptize you in the name of Father, and the Son, and the Holy Spirit." Perhaps you will also be able to hear another voice that is near and yet from beyond, "This is my beloved daughter or son. This child is the apple of my eye." Imagine yourself being held in the everlasting arms of God (*Pause for 20 seconds*) and now imagine God blessing you while keeping you in the holding (*Pause for 20 seconds*) and now imagine God's face shining on you. Take a few moments to give expression in writing to what it means to you to be created in God's image and named as God's child. (*Allow 5–10 minutes for writing*)

Remembering that you are called to live as God's child in the world, imagine what you would look like if the image of God were clearly visible in you . . . what you would say . . . what you would do. Imagine looking at yourself in the mirror and seeing a Christlike image. What do you see? Imagine that your facial expression says exactly what you'd like to communicate to people about the Christ who lives in you. What qualities would people see in you if it were no longer you but Christ in you that they saw? (*Pause for 1 minute*)

Imagine being in the world as a person who fully reflected the image of God. What do you see? What do you want to change in what you see? If you had three wishes to make, what would they be? (*Pause for 1 minute*)

Take a few moments to write from within the experience of being created in the image of God, named as God's child, and called to live as God's child in the world. Let your writing be spontaneous, without any attempt on your part to analyze or censor what you are feeling and thinking. (*Allow 5–10 minutes for writing*)

Making Transitions

This exercise belongs under the category of wellness, because transitions are as normal as the change of seasons. Transitions can be developmental, like leaving home, or situational, like moving from one job to another. Since transitions are as inevitable as change, they are not an indication of illness or lack of wholeness, though inadequate coping with a transition may well lead to brokenness in one's life.

Transitions may be rough or smooth, but even smooth transitions bring changes that cause stress. Stress is related to illness, but not in the sense that a particular event, such as the death of a spouse, is so stressful that it causes illness. It is how one copes with the stress of a transition that determines its relation to illness. The purpose of the following exercise is to use the imagery of faith for dealing with the stress of transitions.

There are three stages to every transition. The first stage is coping with the inevitable loss that comes with an ending. We ignore endings, mostly, and focus on what lies ahead: the next goal, the next job, the next marriage. To ignore endings is to invite stress into our lives, hidden in the unresolved grief that may be expressed in the form of physical and emotional symptoms. The second stage of a transition is like wandering in a wilderness. Nothing is firmly in place. We know where we've been and where we're headed, but there is no clear sense of direction. The confusion of a wilderness journey is normal but unsettling. Only after we have attended to the sense of loss and being lost can we talk about a transition as a new beginning. Things fall into place, and the way into the future becomes clear.

Two striking biblical stories provide powerful imagery for transitions. The first is the journey of the Israelites from Egypt, a place where they had put down deep roots. Their liberation was also a loss, as their desert whining shows.

The wilderness wandering was a long and arduous period of testing, and the challenge of conquering and settling the promised land was obviously not without its stress. The New Testament counterpart to this story is the death and resurrection of Jesus. The ending of his life was hard, and the Gospels make no attempt to soften it. The way of the cross also had the character of a wilderness journey, because it could not have been obvious to Jesus how it was all going to come out. Only after enduring the full terrors of death did Jesus emerge on the other side of the grave as the pioneer of the new creation.

Those doing this exercise will be asked to select a transition that is currently occurring in their lives. It can be one that is just beginning or one that is close to completion. It will be useful to have given some thought to the choice of a particular transition before the beginning of the exercise, though time will be allowed during the exercise for that choice to be made. The transition may be developmental, related to the stage of one's life, or situational, related to matters like job and place of residence.

More than perhaps any other exercise in this book, I would recommend that time be allowed following the exercise for some sharing of experiences. Nobody should be pressured to do that, of course, but there will likely be many within the group who will be grateful for the opportunity.

Guided Imagery

Find as relaxed a position as you can in the chairs where you are sitting, keeping your back straight and your legs uncrossed. Be aware of your breathing as you take several deep breaths, breathing in the breath of life . . . and breathing out tension and stress . . . breathing in the breath of life . . . and breathing out tension and stress . . . breathing in the breath of life . . . and breathing out tension and stress . . . feeling more and more relaxed each time you breathe . . . breathing in the breath of life that comes from God, and breathing out all of the tension and stress that threatens your life with dis-ease.

With the aid of your imagination, go to a place where you can be fully relaxed and by yourself. It may be a favorite place in nature: deep in the woods or on a sandy beach or high up on a mountainside. Or it may be a sacred place that you associate with the presence of God: a church or cathedral or a place of prayer in your home. Or it can be a place that you create and furnish with the aid of your imagination. Go to that place now and feel the goodness of being there. Look with your mind's eye at the surroundings . . . hearing the sounds or enjoying the silence of this place . . . letting the peace and beauty surrounding you gradually still your soul . . . letting all the concerns that seemed so important only a few moments ago lazily drift away like a balloon slowly rising toward the sky . . . feeling yourself becoming more and more relaxed and at peace with yourself . . . with the world . . . and with God. (*Pause for 30 seconds*)

As you relax in this place of peace that invites quiet meditation, reflect for a moment on the transitions in your life: transitions that have not yet been completed, transitions just beginning, or transitions that lie in the near future. There are likely to be many, some much bigger than others. It may be a life-cycle transition, like getting married, having children, or retiring. It may be a transition related to a particular situation, like changing your job or place of residence. It may be a big transition or one of lesser importance. As you think of transitions occurring in your life right now or facing you in the near future, jot them down on the paper in front of you, just a word or a phrase to remind you of a particular transition. After each notation, close your eyes again and return to the special place you have created within the inner world of your experience. (*Pause for 1–2 minutes*) Looking over the list of transitions that you have noted, choose one that you are drawn to, one that invites further reflection. It need not be a major transition or the one you've been most preoccupied with recently. (*Pause for 30 seconds*)

Concentrate first on what it is that you're leaving behind, what it is that's ending. Picture in your mind what you are leaving behind: a face, a place, perhaps something you're doing, whatever represents for you what is ending with this transition. With the aid of your imagination, go to that person or place or activity and say good-bye, but only after you have acknowledged to yourself how much this person or place has meant to you. Whether saying good-bye evokes feelings of relief or regret, remind yourself why this ending is necessary and then say good-bye in whatever way seems most natural to you. Let the experience deepen, and when you are ready, spontaneously express in writing the feelings and thoughts that are triggered by this experience. (*Allow 5 minutes for writing*)

Having said good-bye, focus your attention on the wilderness journey that takes you from where you have been to where you are going. You may not have begun the wilderness portion of your transition, or it may be that it has almost ended. For some of you it will be short; for others of you, very long. Wherever you are in that wilderness journey, search for an image of this time between what has ended and what has not yet begun. The wilderness journey of the Israelites is one such image, a time of wandering where you know where you've been and have some sense of where you are going but feel unsettled and unsure about where you are. Or it may be the image of a ship on a storm-tossed sea, far off course. If no particular image suggests itself, then simply pay attention to the thoughts and feelings that accompany the awareness of being neither here nor there, but rather tenuously situated somewhere in between. When you are ready, let your pen spontaneously express the feelings and thoughts that well up from the experience of being in between. (*Allow 5 minutes for writing*)

Having said good-bye and having faced the necessary journey between what was and what is to come, you are now ready for the possibilities that come with a new beginning. Search for an image of the new beginning: a face, a place, a possibility that awaits you in the future. You may be close enough to the new beginning to have a clear and concrete picture in your mind of the future. But it may be that you will have difficulty in forming any image, so unclear is the shape of the new beginning. You may even feel so trapped in the wilderness journey that hope in the promise of a new beginning seems tenuous. In that case, perhaps something like the dawning of Easter morning will be an appropriate image of a totally unexpected new beginning. It's not a clear picture of a new beginning that is important but a deepening trust in the promise that there will be a new beginning, even if it cannot be clearly discerned right now. I'll give you a moment to let that awareness deepen. (*Pause for 30 seconds*) When you are ready, let your pen express what you are feeling and thinking about the possibilities and the challenges that lie before you. (*Allow 5 minutes for writing*)

Temptations That Threaten Your Health

MATTHEW 4:10

At the very beginning of his ministry, Jesus was tempted to deny his true identity as the chosen one of God. The temptations of Satan were subtle because he seemed to be offering Jesus a way of fulfilling that identity by taking care of his physical welfare, by making a name for himself, and by gaining access to sources of power within the world. Satan plays the role of a pragmatist. He identified human needs (for food, self-esteem, and empowerment) and then suggested practical ways to meet those needs. Jesus recognized, however, the faith question in each of the choices he faced: Whom do you trust? Perhaps after forty days in the desert Satan had become a symbol for self, and the real question was trusting God or trusting himself. Whatever the interpretation of this story, Jesus resisted the temptation and preserved his wellness, his spiritual wellness.

Temptation is not sin, though temptation is a sham if sin is not a possible outcome of the choices one makes. Temptation is a universal human condition that is built into our createdness. To be human is to be finite and insecure. Anxiety is an inevitable consequence of being able to exercise only limited control over our destiny. As a human being, Jesus experienced such existential anxiety, anxiety that is built into human existence and must be resolved by means of faith rather than therapy. Jesus was tempted as we are because he was human. Too much emphasis on Jesus' divinity will sap the power of this story's witness to the human faith of Jesus in resisting temptation.

Our temptations, like those of Jesus, are a threat to our spiritual health. Our temptations are not sin or even a form of spiritual sickness or weakness. Temptations are simply indicators of our humanity and the finitude that is part of our humanity. Borrowing from the contemporary literature on health, we can say that temptations accompany stresses, life situations, or events that tax our capacity to cope effectively. We are tempted to solve our problems by trusting in someone or something other than God. Learning from Jesus how to resist such temptation is the purpose of this exercise.

This exercise focuses on Jesus' temptations as well as our own. Jesus is the model, the "pioneer and perfecter of our faith" (Heb. 12:2). The exercise is designed to facilitate identification with Jesus in his temptation through an inner dialogue with him about it. The three temptations of Jesus provide three general types of temptation, but each person will supply the context that makes the temptations his or her own.

Guided Imagery

Relaxing as well as you can in the chair where you are sitting, feel the tension drain from your muscles as your body becomes more and more at ease and comfortable . . . letting your eyes close to keep distractions away from the inner world that you are about to enter . . . shutting out the noise and the distractions of the outside world and seeking the stillness and peace that this exercise provides you . . . letting your body relax and your imagination float free . . . ridding yourself of all the thoughts that crowd into your consciousness . . . letting them drift away like feathers escaping in the wind . . . letting the quietness still your soul as all distractions of sight and hearing fade away . . . hearing only the sound of my voice as you go deeper into the solitude of your inner being, there to create a place for yourself apart from the noise and distractions of a busy and sometimes stressful life. It can be any place that you choose, perhaps an inner room that you have created for yourself or some special place in nature that comes easily to mind as a sanctuary for you. Go there now and find a place to relax and let the stillness deepen. (*Pause for 1 minute*)

The first temptation of Jesus came in the desert after forty days of fasting. Let your mind float back over the years to a time when you were very hungry, perhaps a day when you had little or nothing to eat, not because you were ill but because you were fasting or dieting or simply without food available. Recall what it was like to be really hungry, so hungry that you couldn't think about anything else, your starving body continually calling your attention to its immediate need. Then imagine what it would be like after two days . . . a week . . . two weeks . . . a month. Jesus was challenged to prove his divinity by creating a loaf of bread, thus satisfying both spiritual and physical needs. Imagine that you are with him and as hungry as he. He asks your counsel. What would you tell him? (*Pause for 30 seconds*)

In your mind's eye put yourself into a situation where you have an immediate and pressing need. Not necessarily food but something you consider essential for your life. (*Pause for 20 seconds*) Imagine a way of satisfying the need that seems plausible but poses a threat to your spiritual health. (*Pause for 20 seconds*) Now imagine that Jesus is there and you seek his counsel. What would he tell you? (*Pause for 20 seconds*) As you feel ready, write for a few moments on whatever comes to your mind when you say, "When I want above all to satisfy my immediate needs . . ." (*Allow 5 minutes for writing*)

The second temptation of Jesus was to jump from the temple roof. The protection he would receive from the holy angels would be proof of divine support for him and his mission. Imagine what it must have been like for Jesus to have the opportunity to perform a spectacular feat that would have ensured instant recognition for him and the mission he was about to undertake. What better evidence of power and authority? What better demonstration of faith? Imagine that you are there with Jesus at the edge of the temple roof. He turns to you and asks for your counsel. What would you say? (*Pause for 20 seconds*)

Call to mind a situation, either past or present, in which you feel anxious about the future and in need of some assurance that God is with you and providing support and direction. It could be a crisis related to a health problem or perhaps a momentous decision about choosing or changing a career. It might be a time of deep depression, self-doubt, or doubting God. (*Pause for 20 seconds*) Whatever the size or type of problem you face, consider the situation in the light of your faith. Is a leap of faith called for? What kind of help are you looking for from God? Imagine that Jesus is with you as you ponder your dilemma. You turn to him and ask for his counsel. What would he say? (*Pause for 20 seconds*) As you are ready, write for a few moments whatever comes to your mind when you think about wanting certainty or proof that what you are doing fits within the plan of God. (*Allow 5 minutes for writing*)

The third temptation of Jesus was the offer of great political power to bring about changes in the world if he would but sell his soul. Remember that Jesus was the son of a carpenter in an obscure part of the world. Imagine what it was like for him to have the opportunity to be at the very center of power in the world of politics and economics. Not for himself, of course, but for what it could mean for the oppressed, for the hungry, for the sick. Imagine that you are there with Jesus and he asks for your counsel. What would you say? (*Pause for 20 seconds*)

Imagine that you've just won the lottery, and it's the biggest sum of money that anybody has ever won. Suddenly your wealth exceeds your wildest dreams. With wealth comes power and influence. Many people approach you with suggestions about how to make use of this newfound wealth. Imagine that Jesus is with you as you ponder the future. You turn to him and ask for his counsel. What does he say? (*Pause for 20 seconds*)

As you are ready, write whatever comes to your mind when you think of what you would do with great wealth and power. (*Allow 5 minutes for writing*)

Bring your writing to a close, and as you are ready, return to this room renewed and refreshed for your spiritual journey.

The Body as
Temple of the Holy Spirit

This exercise was originally prepared for a senior citizens group, but it can be used by any individual or group. There are advantages and disadvantages to using guided imagery with older adults. The advantage is that people are likely to be much more thoughtful and reflective as they move into the retirement years. They are not as likely to be preoccupied with the incessant demands that are placed on people who are fully employed and raising a family. Furthermore, they are more deeply attuned to spiritual concerns. A disadvantage is that some individuals may be suspicious of a technique that is foreign to their experience. Another disadvantage is that the relaxation that is induced to facilitate imagery may more readily induce sleep than it would in someone younger and likely to be under more stress. For that reason, the relaxation portion of the following exercise is slightly shorter than with other exercises.

The focus of this exercise is on awareness of the body. The older we are, the more aware we are likely to be of bodily functions. The body of an elderly person cannot be taken for granted in the way a young person's often can. Older people are more likely to view their bodies as dialogical partners than as slaves to do their bidding.

The guiding metaphor for body in this exercise is the temple of the Holy Spirit. We would do well to think of a regular and willful desecration of the human body as a sin against the Holy Spirit. Seeing our bodies as apt vessels for the presence of the Holy Spirit provides the basis for an experiential appreciation of the body and for the renewal of a commitment to the care of the body.

Guided Imagery

Generally, imagery works best if you have your feet flat on the floor and your back straight, but only if that is a comfortable position for you. Be as relaxed as you can where you are sitting, letting yourself settle comfortably into your chair. Close your eyes or keep them focused on one place in the room so that you can direct your attention to what is going on inside you rather than being distracted by me or anything else. We spend most of our waking hours attending to people and events outside us and precious little time paying attention to our bodies and what is going on inside us.

Be aware of your breathing . . . letting your breathing come slowly and naturally . . . gradually attuning yourself to the internal rhythm of your body . . . breathing in energy and new life . . . breathing out tension and worry . . . letting yourself be drawn naturally and slowly toward the inner world of your experience . . . becoming more and more relaxed . . . moving into the inner chambers of your body . . . becoming aware of your body from within rather than seeing it as a mirror image, something external to you. (*Pause for 20 seconds*)

Imagine that you have come upon a door that is deep inside the inner chambers of your body. A sign over the door reads, Temple of the Holy Spirit. Opening the door, you enter a place that is dark except for a gleaming white altar which glows with a soft, subdued light. Aware that this is a sacred place within yourself in the same way that a church is a sacred place in the outer world, approach the altar. In any way that seems appropriate to you, acknowledge the presence of God in this sacred place within the inner chambers of your body. (*Pause for 1 minute*)

From within this sacred place called the Temple of the Holy Spirit, take a few moments to reflect on the wonder of your body and how well it functions. In your mind's eye picture your heart beating without any effort on your part, beating regularly when you are awake and when you are asleep, beating faster when your body needs more oxygen and slower when you are at rest. Imagine hearing the words "Gift of God" echoing in your mind as you observe the effortless working of your heart. Hear those words repeated again and again in rhythm with your heartbeat: "Gift of God, Gift of God, Gift of God." (*Pause for 20 seconds*) In your mind's eye go to other places in your body where you can observe your seeing, your hearing, your thinking, in each place hearing the words "Gift of God." I'll give you a moment to complete that journey through your body. (*Pause for 1 minute*)

Still within the sacred place that you have created with your imagination, let your mind drift back over the years to times when you have failed to treat your body as the temple of the Holy Spirit. Remember times when you have abused your body, perhaps through the use of alcohol or tobacco, perhaps by eating too much food, perhaps by not getting enough sleep or exercise, perhaps by subjecting your body to excessive stress. I'll give you a moment to remember times when you have abused your body. (*Pause for 30 seconds*) Remembering that your body is the temple of the Holy Spirit, confess to God all the times that you have treated your body as anything but holy and ask forgiveness from both God and your body. (*Pause for 30 seconds*) With your mind's ear, hear the word of forgiveness spoken by God especially to you, absolving you of all your sins toward your body. (*Pause for 30 seconds*)

Be aware of present infirmities in your body, places of tension and discomfort, perhaps places of chronic pain. Be aware of losses you have suffered: loss of hearing or sight, loss of mobility, loss of memory and ability to concentrate, loss of function in some part of your body. Be aware of any messages from your body that something is not right. (*Pause for 30 seconds*) In your mind's eye imagine the healing power of the Holy Spirit moving through your body to the places of dis-ease that you have noted and bringing relief to those places of suffering. You can imagine that healing energy as intense white light or as warm, soothing water or in any other form that your imagination suggests. I will give you a moment to visualize the healing power of the Spirit of God at work within your body. (*Pause for 1 minute*)

Aware of your body as the temple of the Holy Spirit, take a moment to form a covenant with your body by making a promise to be a better caretaker of your body in the future. Try to be as specific as you can in stating what it is that you will do to provide better care for your body. (*Pause for 1 minute*)

Imagine now that you have died, and this temple of the Holy Spirit that is your body is transformed into a spiritual body fit for the resurrection. Imagine this in any way you wish as long as your body remains a body, however different from the one you know so intimately in the present. Imagine your spiritual body as whole, healthy, and full of energy, radiating with the presence and power of the risen Christ within. Sense the close connection between the spiritual body you will have in the resurrection and the body you have now, which Jesus calls the temple of the Holy Spirit. Reflect for a moment on the transformation of your physical body to a spiritual body. (*Pause for 30 seconds*)

As you are ready, gradually return from your journey inward and reorient yourself to this place and time, refreshed and renewed in body and spirit, feeling the power and presence of God within you.

Freedom in Christ

The freedom we experience as Christians comes through Christ, whose death and resurrection frees us to be the people that God intends us to be. Christ not only frees us from sin through forgiveness, as important as that is to our new life in Christ; he also frees us from illness, as the healing stories of the Gospels illustrate again and again. In addition, there are resources in the Gospels that help us to remain free. Wellness exercises in this chapter, like "Imaging the Image of God," are designed with that purpose in mind.

The following exercise is designed to enable people to draw on their resources of faith to gain freedom from different kinds of bondage in their lives and to use that freedom for the care of others. What distinguishes this exercise on freedom from one that might be done in a secular setting is the assumption that it is Christ who frees and unites.

This exercise offers a variety of ways that one might experience "freedom in Christ." As written, it is too long for most occasions other than a workshop. However, some sections of the exercise can be easily deleted.

Guided Imagery

Close your eyes so that your attention will be directed inward instead of on what is going on outside you. Relax and release whatever tension you feel in your body . . . letting the tension within you flow down and out of your body like newly melted snow flowing down a mountain stream. Pay attention to your breathing and its natural rhythm . . . attuning yourself to that rhythm and becoming more and more relaxed . . . letting your mind be as free of worry as your body is free of tension . . . letting any thoughts or sounds that intrude into your consciousness simply float by until they are past, like distant clouds that come and go . . . giving yourself the freedom to explore the inner world of your experience . . . letting the sound of my voice guide you gradually and gently further and further into a state of deep peacefulness . . . feeling more and more relaxed as you release all the tensions and worries that have been burdening you.

Imagine yourself in some pleasant place that you can easily create with the aid of your imagination. It can be any place that you choose, maybe a favorite place in the woods or by a lake or stream. Make it a safe place, a place where you will not be bothered, a place that is relaxing and peaceful. Find a comfortable spot there to lie or sit . . . letting the peacefulness of the setting deepen the peacefulness that you feel inside of yourself. (*Pause for 20 seconds*)

Focus your attention on any physical impediments that bind or limit you in some way, impediments that keep you from feeling fit, that hinder your service to others, that sour your disposition. It need not be a major impediment, such as a physical disability or chronic illness. It will more likely be something minor, something that is a constant source of irritation, such as a persistent allergy, lower back pain, headaches, or a gradual hearing loss. Choose one such bodily impediment that is a burden to you, that shackles your soul in some way. If you can, form an image of this impediment in your mind's eye. Lower back pain may feel like a knotted rope stretched tight. Throbbing headaches may feel like a drum beating in your head. If no image is forthcoming, simply concentrate on the burdensomeness of this impediment. (*Pause for 30 seconds*)

Now imagine that your whole being—body, mind, and spirit—is surrounded by and filled with the presence of Christ, letting the words of Saint Paul deepen that experience: "It is no longer I who live, but Christ who lives in me" . . . . . "It is no longer I who live, but Christ who lives in me" . . . . . Imagine Christ freeing you from the burden of your physical impediment in any way that seems appropriate and realistic. You might imagine Jesus untying the knot of your lower back pain or silencing the drumbeat of your headache or stilling the storm of an agitated stomach. If removing the impediment seems impossible or unrealistic to you, imagine the negative feelings generated by this ailment being dissipated. Let the experience happen naturally, with no attempt on your part to force it. (*Pause for 30 seconds*)

Shift your awareness to some particular sin or defect in character that binds you, that keeps you from being the person God intends you to be. Choose something you've struggled with for a long time, perhaps addiction of some kind or a personal weakness. Choose something that you feel enslaved by, so that acts of the will, however well intentioned, seem ineffective. Picture in your mind whatever enslaves you, perhaps a bottle or a cigarette or food. Try to push that picture out of your mind, only to have it come back again and again, haunting you with its tempting appeal. (*Pause for 30 seconds*)

Imagine yourself in a prison cell, the prison symbolizing whatever is enslaving you. Picture Christ coming into that cell and sitting across from you. In your mind's eye, imagine the two of you together picking up a bottle, a pack of cigarettes, a piece of food, or whatever it is that enslaves you. What are you expecting from Christ? What are you expecting from yourself? What do you and Christ do with the bottle, the pack of cigarettes, or the food that you are both holding? Let the experience deepen, and when you feel ready, write whatever comes to your mind at the words "What Christ and I will do together about my enslavement is . . ." (*Allow 5 minutes for writing*)

Choose a relationship that has become a burden to you because of the demands it places on you, demands that at times may seem excessive. This could be the burden of caring for a small child or an elderly parent. It could be the burden of being a good listener to someone who turns to you regularly for counsel. It could be the burden felt by a professional care giver whose vocation is meeting the needs of others. (*Pause for 30 seconds*)

In your mind's eye imagine Christ removing this burden from you in any way that seems appropriate. He may take it from your shoulders and place it on his own. He may fill you with renewed energy through his life-giving Spirit. He may lead you to a place full of delight, a place set aside for your renewal. He may support you in your weariness. Whatever image comes, let Christ free you from burdens that have become heavy and draining. As you feel ready, write whatever is in your heart as you reflect on the experience of being freed from an oppressive burden. (*Allow 5 minutes for writing*)

Bring your writing to a close and gradually reorient yourself to the here and now, feeling refreshed and free to be the kind of person Christ has called you to be.

Chapter 5

Exercises for General Use

The exercises in this chapter are a general assortment, and you will need to scan the content of each in order to determine possible use. Three of the exercises use the healing light of Christ as a theme. Two of the exercises take a ritual form, one of blessing and the other of healing. One of the exercises is based on a ritual of deep significance to all Christians, the sacrament of baptism. One of the exercises uses the healing hands of Jesus as a theme, another is a dialogue with one's body about illness and health, and yet another on healing the wounded child within.

Discovering Wholeness
in the Waters of Baptism

Introduction

The sacraments are resources for healing and the maintenance of wholeness in the lives of Christians, both individually and corporately. That is perfectly obvious if we are talking about the healing of the soul or spiritual healing. Both baptism and the Eucharist (sacraments by almost everybody's definition) mediate the forgiveness of sins and nurture the spiritual health of God's people. It's not so obvious to most people that the sacraments are also resources for physcial healing. The model of health and healing that informs these exercises (biopsychospiritual) makes this more intelligible. Physical and spiritual healing have an interactive relationship; what happens at one level of the system affects every other level of the system.

In what ways can we say that baptism is a resource for healing and wholeness? In straightforward spiritual language, sin is a spiritual malady, and baptism is for the forgiveness of sins. Even more important from the spiritual perspective is the confidence that sickness can do its worst in the body, ravaging it to the point of death, yet not affect one's wholeness as a child of God. Indeed, it can be an occasion for becoming whole. The remembering of baptism is a particularly valuable resource in caring for the dying, for baptism is dying with Christ and rising to a new life that cannot be touched by death.

But more than this can be said from a biopsychospiritual perspective. If as baptized Christians we are in Christ or Christ is in us (Saint Paul puts it both ways), then Christ is in us completely, body and soul. This offers assurance not only that we are not alone but also that Christ is *in* the illness—suffering it with us, healing us, and also dying with us. This won't make much sense if you think it's only your body that is sick and not you as a person. But if *you* are sick and you are in Christ, then he is present in your body as well as your soul.

Faith as trust has its deepest roots in baptism, especially infant baptism, for nowhere is the grace of God more clearly evident. We are named as God's childen and promised the enduring love and presence of God along before we can respond in any personal way to this wonderful gift. In times of crisis such as physical illness, trust is the most important element of faith. It is natural in such times, therefore, to return to our roots, our birthing as children of God, to find healing and renewal in the waters of baptism.

How can you remember your baptism if you were baptized as an infant? It calls for a creative act of the imagination. All of our remembering is imaginative in that we rely on images to recall events and creative in that we never simply reproduce the experience we had earlier, even if it was just an hour ago. Returning to an event that we cannot remember but is at the core of our identity as children of God can be a deeply meaningful experience of spiritual and physical renewal.

Guided imagery is a tool for making our baptism experientially rich and meaningful. Most people will be able to imagine their baptism with relative ease (sixteen of eighteen in the group that tested this exercise). The purpose of this exercise is to link the remembering of baptism and the wholeness it brings to the experience of illness. It is designed for use in the spiritual care of the sick, including the care of oneself. It can be easily adapted for use in a group.

The exercise can be used exactly as written, but it will be much more effective when applied to the individual needs of the person who is sick. The dying have needs that are different from the critically or chronically ill. For example, I would include more of the imagery from Rom. 6:3–5 for a person who is dying. The length of the exercise, the kind of imagery used, and the amount of conversation during the exercise will vary from person to person. I am assuming that the person was baptized as an infant. Adjustments can be easily made for someone who was baptized as an adult. The exercise includes the making of the sign of the cross on

the forehead; this could be distracting to a person not familiar with this liturgical practice.

Guided Imagery

Find a comfortable position in the chair where you are sitting [or bed where you are lying] and consciously relax the
muscles in your body, beginning with the top of your head
down to the bottom of your feet . . . gradually letting the
tension fade away until you feel as relaxed and limp as an
old rag doll . . . resting quietly and calmly . . . letting your
breathing come slowly and regularly . . . letting your inner
self become as still as a lake that mirrors the woods behind
it . . . letting your worries and fears about your illness flow
from you as rainwater flows from the roof of a house . . .
finding deep within yourself a center that is a place of quiet
and tranquillity far removed from the disorder and disruption you feel from the disease . . . letting thoughts become
less turbulent and feelings less intense.

Though you were not old enough to remember your
baptism as an infant, use your imagination to go back to the
day of your baptism and picture it in your mind's eye. Picture a church setting, either the actual church where you
were batized or one that you create in your imagination
right now. Picture the worship setting in which your baptism takes place, perhaps a church service or maybe just
a large family gathering. Imagine yourself being held securely in the arms of someone you trust. It might be your
mother, your father, a godparent, or anyone that you would
want to hold you. Feel how good it is to be held securely
by someone who holds you well, someone you trust. Think
of the people you would like to be there, people you know
now as well as people who would have known you then.
You can decide who should be there. Select people who
have nurturned and sustained you in your identity as a child
of God. Imagine them all surrounding the font or place
of baptism as part of a large family gathering. (*Pause for
1 minute*)

Imagine the pastor [priest] that you would like to baptize
you. It can be the person who actually did baptize you or
it can be a pastor [priest] of your own choosing, someone
you know now or someone in the past who is a wisdom

figure for you. Feel the touch on your forehead as the sign of the cross is made, reminding you that you have been redeemed by Christ. Feel the water being poured over your head, or imagine what it might be like to be fully immersed in water. Hear the words that are spoken as the water flows over your body: "I baptize you in the name of the Father, and the Son, and the Holy Spirit." (*Pause for 30 seconds*)

Feel the cleansing that comes with the washing of the water and the promise of forgiveness. Hear the word of promise assuring you that nothing that could possibly happen to you would ever leave you all alone. Sense the presence of the risen Christ all around you. Sense that presence flowing in you and through you until you can say, "It is no longer I who live but Christ who lives in me." (*Pause for 20 seconds*)

Feel the energy of the new life that is God's gift to you. Feel its power, its permanence, its immortality. Let a sense of your oneness with the risen Christ grow in your heart and transport you beyond the grasp of your suffering, beyond the worries and terrors that fill your waking days and haunt your dreams, beyond the sin-sick existence that makes your soul heavy and weary. (*Pause for 20 seconds*)

Feel the safety, the security, and the reassurance that comes with the experience of being baptized. Imagine yourself being held securley by the everlasting arms of God as you listen to a voice speaking in the same soothing tone that a mother would use with her child: "You are baptized. You are baptized. Nothing can separate you from my love which is in Christ and embedded deeply within you. You are baptized. You are my beloved child. I will always be with you." (*Pause for 30 seconds*)

As you feel ready, return from this experience to where we are now, feeling refreshed and renewed by the healing waters of your baptism.

(*Conclude the session with a brief discussion about the meaning of his or her baptism in relation to the experience of illness, concluding with a prayer that flows out of that discussion.*)

Imagery Rituals
of Blessing and Healing

Introduction

We look to God for both blessing and healing. The blessing of God comes with our birth and is built into the order of creation. All living things are gifted with what Matthew Fox aptly calls the "original blessing" of God. The sun and rain are blessing of God, the air that we breathe, and the food that we eat. The wondrous working of our bodies (hearing, seeing, tasting, feeling, and thinking) is a blessing of God. We would continue to need the blessing of God even if we lived in a perfect creation where there was no sin, no sickness, no pain, no death. For without the continued blessing of God, there would be no continuing creation. In spite of their limited cosmology, the ancient Hebrews were right in believing that the sun comes up in the morning because God so commands. That is equally true for everything in nature, everything from the broadest reaches of cosmic space to the innermost regions of subatomic particles. All is dependent on God's continual blessing.

Rituals of healing are needed because the original blessing is continually marred by what Christians call original sin. The world as we know it is mixed with blessing and curse, health and illness, salvation and sin. Rituals of healing are needed because our world lacks wholeness at every level of existence. Individuals lack wholeness in body, mind, and spirit. Families splinter from lack of a shared vision and common commitment. The earth is wounded, and we wound it more every day. Relationships at the national, international, and personal levels are threatened by distrust and selfish interests. Thus we yearn for healing as well as blessing with a dream of nothing less than the mending of all creation as our hope.

Imagery and ritual are combined in the exercises for blessing and for healing. The exercises are designed for use in a group, but they can be adapted for use with only two persons. In each of the exercises, individuals will pair off within the larger group. The leader will begin the exercise with guided imagery for the whole group and then guide the individual paris in a mutual exchange of blessing or healing. Participants need to be fully informed about the process before the exercise begins. That will allow individuals to opt out of the exercise if they feel uncomfortable with it, and it will eliminate the need for giving instructions on logistics in the middle of the exercise.

Those doing the exercise should be paired off and seated next to each other before the exercise begins. They should be told in advance that each partner will be instructed during the exercise to place hands on his or her partner's head, saying "God's blessing for you" or "God's healing for you," and then making the sign of the cross on the partner's forehead. The sign of the cross can be eliminated if that is not a familiar ritual sign to members of the group. Those doing the exercise should be given permission to add additional words of blessing and healing if that seems appropriate, but most people will prefer the simple phrase. Before beginning the exercise, give people the opportunity to ask their partners if they have need of a particular blessing or healing. Go over these instructions at least twice, giving a step-by-step procedure of what will happen in the ritual process and then asking if there are any questions.

Every effort should be made to minimize any awkwardness, although some will feel uncomfortable even with the minimal ritual in this exercise. Partners will need to decide who should go first. Suggest that they open their eyes while giving the blessing but keep them closed while receiving the blessing. After the exchange of blessing, the ritual will close with a mutual laying on of hands.

Most people will want to do these exercises with someone they know well and feel comfortable with. However, there may be advantages to a random selection of pairs when static between a married couple or friends would pose a barrier to full participation in the exercise. Another advantage of random selection is that it broadens the sense of the church as people called to give and receive blessing and healing within the entire community and not just within a small circle of family and friends.

EXERCISE 1, IMAGERY RITUAL OF BLESSING

Guided Imagery

Notice any place within your body that may be tense. Loosen the muscles in that area through gentle movement, like rotating your neck or stretching your muscles. Feel your body become more relaxed, and, as you are ready, close your eyes . . . letting the quietness deepen within yourself . . . letting your breathing come more slowly and evenly . . . allowing whatever tension remains in your body to drain away . . . letting the stillness enter your soul . . . letting the breath come more slowly and evenly . . . allowing yourself to drift slowly down the well of your interior self, as slowly as a leaf falling from a tree in autumn, drifting slowly toward the center of your inner being, there to explore freely the pathways of your mind, open to you when you allow yourself time for interior reflection. (*Pause for 20 seconds*)

Sense the wonder of life within you, life that came bursting from the womb and is ever growing and developing into the person you are. Imagine your life as a journey down a stream that has very small beginnings but gradually widens and deepens as new sources of experience and learning are added. Picture yourself floating down that strem from the time you were born until now, a stream that is broad and smooth in some parts and full of boulders and turbulent waters in other places. As you float down the stream of your life, recall the faces of persons who have blessed you in some special way on your journey, persons who have nurtured you and guided you, who have picked you up when you've fallen down and cared for you when you were not well.

Single out five or six people in your life who have blessed you in such a way, perhaps by keeping you safe or guiding you well or bringing delight into your life. Jot down the initials of these persons, along with a phrase that suggests the way the person has been a blessing to you, opening your eyes just long enough to make the notation on paper. (*Pause for 2 minutes*)

After you've looked over the list of people who have been a blessing to you, choose one of them and recall a time in your life when you were particularly aware of the blessing this person brought to you, perhaps because of the vividness with which you recall this time or perhaps because it was such an original blessing and has had significance for all that has happened to you since then. (*Pause for 30 seconds*)

Reenter that experience with the aid of your imagination and let the blessing unfold once again. What did the person say or do that was important to you? What difference has it made since then? How would you be different if you hadn't received this special blessing? Were you aware then or are you aware now of God being the source of the blessing you received from this person? Construct for yourself an image of God blessing you, perhaps through a light from above radiating through this person to you. (*Pause for 30 seconds*)

Can you recall a time when you were able to provide a similar kind of blessing to another person? Reenter that experience with the aid of your imagination, and feel the goodness of blessing someone else through what you said or did. Are you aware of God being the source of the blessing you give? Construct an image of God blessing this person through you, or just sense a love or power greater than yourself flowing through you. (*Pause for 30 seconds*)

God continues to bless us through the blessings of others, though we are often oblivious to the ultimate source of blessing. Give and receive the blessing of God by turning to your partner, placing your hand firmly on his or her head, saying his or her name along with a word of blessing like "The blessing of God for you." Complete the blessing with the sign of the cross on your partner's forehead. After the exchange of blessings, both of you place your hands on the head of your partner, close your eyes and feel the presence and power of God radiating through your whole being, body and spirit. Proceed with the blessing. (*Allow 1 minute of silence after the blessings have been exchanged*)

With your eyes still closed, withdraw your hands from the head of your partner and meditate in silence on the experience of giving and receiving the blessing of God in your life. As you feel ready, express in writing what this experience was like. As a heading, write "Giving and Receiving the Blessing of God." Then write whatever is in your heart, letting the words flow spontaneously from your pen without analysis or critique of what you are thinking and feeling. (*Allow 5–10 minutes for writing*)

EXERCISE 2, IMAGERY RITUAL OF HEALING

Guided Imagery

Notice any place within your body that may be tense. Loosen the muscles in that area through gentle movement, like rotating your neck or stretching your muscles. Feel your body become more relaxed, and, as you are ready, close your eyes . . . letting the quietness deepen within yourself . . . letting your breathing come more slowly and evenly . . . allowing whatever tension remains in your body to drain away . . . letting the stillness enter your soul . . . letting the breath come more slowly and evenly . . . allowing yourself to drift slowly down the well of your interior self, as slowly as a leaf falling from a tree in autumn, drifting slowly toward the center of your inner being, there to explore freely the pathways of your mind, open to you when you allow yourself time for interior reflection. (*Pause for 20 seconds*)

Sense the wonder of life within you, life that came bursting from the womb and is ever growing and developing into the person you are. Imagine your life as a journey down a stream that has very small beginnings but gradually widens and deepens as new sources of experience and learning add to it. Imagine the stream of your life as being broad and smooth in some parts and full of boulders and turbulent waters in other places . . .

Remembering those times in the stream of your life when you were in turbulent waters, recall five or six occasions when you were in need of rescue or healing, times when the turbulence and chaos seemed overwhelming, times when you were ill-at-ease or hurt in body, mind, or spirit . . . As you recall such troubled times, let images of people who have rescued you or healed you come to mind, and jot down a word or phrase that captures the feeling of that time. This need not be a major rescue mission; it might have been only a passing remark or small act of kindness, but something that has become symbolically significant to you. (*Pause for 2 minutes*)

Looking over your list, choose one occasion when you feel like you were rescued or healed. With the aid of your imagination reenter that experience. Why was this such an important event? How were you helped? Could anyone else have done what this person did? How is your life different because of it? Try to form an image of God as the source of your healing or rescue, perhaps in the form of a halo on the head of the person who helped you or sensing Christ's presence in the look or the touch of this person . . . . . Then imagine yourself as a person with a healing touch, a healing look, a person through whom Christ can heal others. As you are ready, write for a few moments about your experience of being healed and being a healer. (*Allow 5 minutes for writing*)

God continues to heal us through others and to heal others through us, though we are often oblivious to the ultimate source of healing. Give and receive God's own healing by turning to your partner, placing your hands firmly on his or her head, and saying, "God's healing for you." You may personalize this prayer for healing by relating it to some particular wound or hurt if that is appropriate, though it is not necessary. After you've said the prayer for healing, make the sign of the cross on the person's forehead. After the exchange of healing prayer, both of you place your hands on the forehead of your partner, close your eyes, and feel the healing presence of God radiating through your body, mind, and spirit. Proceed when you are ready. (*Allow 1 minute of silence after the exchange of healing prayers*)

With your eyes still closed, withdraw your hands from the head of your partner and reflect on the experience of giving and receiving the healing power of God in your life. As you feel ready, express in writing what this experience was like. Was it easier to give or receive a prayer for healing? Which made the greatest impact on you? What did you learn about yourself in this experience? (*Allow 5–10 minutes for writing*)

The Healing Light of Christ

The following exercises use light as a means for imaging the healing presence and power of Christ. The use of light as a metaphor for the presence of Christ flows directly from the New Testament description of Jesus, much of it Jesus' own description of himself. In the Gospel of John Jesus frequently refers to himself as "the light of the world" (9:5, 12:1, 12:35–36, 12:46). Saint Paul carries the metaphor further by saying to the Ephesian Christians, in the Lord you are light. "Now in the Lord you are light. Live as children of light" (5:8) The light comes from beyond us as a gift: "Every generous act of giving, with every perfect gift, is from above, coming down from the Father of lights, with whom there is no variation or shadow due to change" (James 1:17).

Light is not the only image that can be used to convey the presence of a transcendent reality, though it is the most common. The images of fire (Pentecost, the burning bush) or of breath (inspiration of the Holy Spirit, breathing life into Adam) also convey the presence of God in powerful ways. But the universality of the image of light in religions, attested by those who report near-death experiences from many cultures, suggests how deeply it is embedded in the human psyche.

There is a difference between using light as a metaphor and using it in the form of imagery. Light as a metaphor is a figure of speech containing an implied comparison, while in imagery one is asked to form a mental picture of light to enhance the experience of Christ's presence. Both the image and the metaphor of light gain their expressive power through the spiritual qualities of light: enabling sight, generating warmth, engendering life, coming from beyond, and so forth. Like the metaphor, the use of the image in no way implies that the light *is* Christ, but imagery is more than a figure of speech and is likely to facilitate a much more powerful experience of the presence of Christ than the use of a metaphor.

There are three separate exercises in this section: the healing light of Christ for oneself, the healing light of Christ for others, and healing light at the end of the rainbow.

The following paragraphs suggest how these exercises might be introduced to a group.

> We construct images in the same way that we construct words, to make sense out of our experience. The only difference is that words are abstract while images are much more concrete and close to experience. They are also more imaginative and spontaneously generated, as in dreams. You can create any kind of image you want in your mind's eye, as you probably have in your daydreams. The kind of image that I'm going to suggest you use during this exercise is the image of Christ as light that surrounds you and is in you.
>
> Why the image of light? Because it's true to Scripture and because it can be a powerful expression of our experience of God. The most natural way to imagine the presence of Christ in a guided imagery exercise is to picture him as the person you've come to know from the stories in the Gospels. But sometimes Scripture suggests other ways to imagine the presence of Christ in our lives. For example, the imagery of light seems especially appropriate for what Saint Paul talks about when he says that we are "in Christ" or that Christ is in us. When Paul says, "It is no longer I who live, but Christ who lives in me," it doesn't make much sense to think of a tiny little person inside you. "Light" or "energy" seems to be a much more appropriate expression of our experience, especially since Jesus himself uses it when he says, "I am the light of the world." So if you've never imagined Christ as light before, give yourself permission to do so now as a way of deepening your experience of Christ being within you.

EXERCISE 1, HEALING LIGHT FOR ONESELF
Guided Imagery

Let all the tension that has collected in your muscles from the stresses and strains of the day drain slowly away as you settle yourself comfortably in the chair where you are sitting. Take several deep breaths, and as you exhale feel all the accumulated tension in your body flow away. As you relax your body, let your eyelids close, or keep your eyes focused on one particular place in order to avoid distractions. Beginning with the top of your head, visualize the tension that remains there as drops of water forming a trickle and then a stream that is slowly flowing down from your shoulders and arms and chest and every portion of your body until it all drains out the bottom of your feet . . . . . As the tension flows away from your body, feel yourself becoming more and more relaxed, more and more in tune with the natural rhythm of your body, which is the rhythm of your breathing . . . breathing in fresh air and life-giving oxygen . . . breathing out stale air and tension . . . breathing in . . . and breathing out . . . slowly and evenly.

Imagine that you are resting comfortably in the warm sun on a secluded beach in the late afternoon. The warmth of the sun feels like a healing balm on your body, and the sound of the gentle surf in the background deepens your feeling of comfort and relaxation. Let your breathing come slowly and evenly, as natural and regular as the surf that gently washes up on the shore. I'll give you a moment to deepen your feeling of relaxation as you feel the healing warmth of the sun's light and listen to the quiet sounds of the surf on the seashore. (*Pause for 1 minute*)

In your mind's eye, visualize the rays of the sun in any way that seems right to you, perhaps as you see them filtered through trees or as they appear when the sun rises or sets . . . seeing the sun's rays infusing life-giving energy into trees and other plants, which seem to stretch out toward the sun to gather in that energy . . . feeling the life-giving power of the sun's rays . . . finding in those rays an image of the healing energy of the light of Christ, the light of the world. The light of Christ radiating love . . . and life . . . and healing. Imagine seeing the light of Christ beaming on you with intensity and brightness without blinding your eyes. Feeling the warmth and love that emanates from this light, you are drawn toward it as if it were a powerful magnet, pulling you effortlessly to the light that you know to be the warm and loving presence of Christ.

Imagine the light wrapped around you like a blanket . . . experiencing the warm and healing presence of Christ as a blanket of light enveloping you on every side, from the tip of your head to the bottom of your feet. (*Pause for 30 seconds*) Imagine this healing and revitalizing light of Christ not only surrounding you like a blanket but flowing through you, bathing and revitalizing every cell of your body. As you hear the words "The Lord is my light and my salvation," experience the healing light moving through you: through every muscle, every blood vessel, every bone, every organ of your body . . . feeling the presence of Christ within you as a powerful healing force penetrating into the farthest corners of your being . . . filling you with the healing and life-giving energy of the new creation that is God's gift to you . . . creating balance and health at every level of your being. (*Pause for 1 minute*)

Focus your attention on any part of your body that has been a source of discomfort to you: a headache, a persistent pain, a dull ache, or some part of your body that you know to be diseased. Imagine the healing light of Christ focused on this part of your body as if it were a laser beam concentrating all of its energy on one location . . . keeping the beam of light focused on that one location . . . perhaps feeling a tingling in that part of your body . . . knowing that it is the will of Christ that you be well, just as it was when he healed the sick who came to him . . . experiencing his healing power in the light that surrounds you and fills you and touches you wherever there is pain and suffering. Take a moment to experience deeply the healing light focusing its energy on any part of your body or mind in need of healing and revitalization. (*Pause for 2 minutes*)

Gradually return to your normal level of consciousness . . . sensing the inner harmony and peace that fills your being . . . your body bathed in the healing light of Christ . . . your spirit radiating the light of Christ that glows from within you. Gradually and gently bring yourself back to this room, alert, and filled with the light and love of the risen Christ. As you feel ready, open your eyes.

EXERCISE 2, HEALING LIGHT FOR OTHERS

Introduction

This exercise is a meditative form of healing prayer. The intent is to deepen the experience of prayer. Even though research seems to support the hypothesis that prayer for the healing of others "works" (results in greater improvement for patients who receive intercessory prayer than for those who don't), those doing the exercise should not be given the impression that they can effect changes in others through what they imagine. The purpose of all intercessory prayer is to bring our needs and hopes before the throne of God, trusting in God's power, not our own. No special claims are made for this kind of prayer. Its chief value is that it facilitates a deep expression of love and compassion on the part of the person who is praying. That doesn't make the prayer "better," but it may make it more meaningful.

Guided Imagery

Let all the tension that has collected in your muscles from the stresses and strains of the day drain slowly away as you settle yourself comfortably in the chair where you are sitting. Take several deep breaths, and as you exhale feel all the accumulated tension in your body flow away. As you relax your body, let your eyelids close or keep your eyes focused on one particular place in order to avoid distractions. Beginning with the top of your head, visualize the tension that remains in your muscles as drops of water forming a trickle and then a stream slowly flowing down from your shoulders and arms and chest and every portion of your body until it all drains out the bottom of your feet . . . As the tension flows away from your body, you will become more and more relaxed, more and more in tune with the natural rhythm of your breathing.

Imagine that you are resting comfortably in the warm sun at whatever location you choose, perhaps a secluded beach in the late afternoon of a summer day or on the deck of a summer cottage. Next to you is the person that you wish to bring into the healing presence of our Lord. Picture the person for whom you are praying in his or her present condition, but pain-free for the moment and able to enjoy the warmth of the sun and the beauty of the surroundings. Let your breathing come slowly and evenly, and imagine the same calm and gentle breathing for the person next to you. Feel the goodness of being there with someone you care about. Sense the closeness of the bond that binds you together as fellow human beings and children of God. (*Pause for 1 minute*)

In your mind's eye, visualize a beam of light like the rays of the sun, a beam of light full of warmth and healing that envelopes you, covering you like a blanket. As you hear the words "I am the light of the world," imagine the beam of healing light to be the presence of the risen Christ. The beam of healing light radiates the warmth of Christ's love for you and all people, and especially for those who are ill. Picture the light as intensely bright without blinding your eyes. Imagine the light filling your whole being, flooding your mind and renewing your spirit, flowing through every portion of your body, removing all tension, pain, and suffering, and bringing balance, harmony, and renewed vitality. Take a moment to deepen the sense of the healing light of Christ flowing into you and through you. (*Pause for 1 minute*)

Imagine that you are a channel of God's healing presence and power to the person for whom you wish to pray. In your mind's eye, place your hands on the head of this person or on that part of his or her body where the injury or disease is located. As you do so, envision the beam of healing light going through your hands into the person you are bringing into the healing presence of Christ. Imagine the beam of light flooding into every corner of this person's body, mind, and spirit. Feel the energizing power of this light as it passes through you and into the body of the person for whom you are praying. Imagine the healing light of Christ being focused on places of dis-ease, discomfort, and disharmony, enabling the person to relax and feel at ease. When you have completed this portion of your healing prayer, follow the same procedure for anyone else in need of your prayer for healing. I will give you several minutes to complete this process. (*Pause for 3 minutes*)

As you are ready, slowly and gently return to this room, feeling refreshed and whole in body, mind, and spirit.

EXERCISE 3, HEALING LIGHT AT THE END OF THE RAINBOW
Guided Imagery

Let all the tension that has collected in your muscles from the stresses and strains of the day drain slowly away as you settle yourself comfortably in the chair where you are sitting. Take several deep breaths, and as you exhale feel all the accumulated tension in your body flow alway. As you relax your body, let your eyelids close or keep your eyes focused on one particular place in order to avoid distractions. Beginning with the top of your head, visualize whatever tension that remains in your muscles as drops of water forming a trickle and then a stream slowly flowing down from your shoulders and arms and chest and every portion of your body until it all drains out the bottom of your feet . . . As the tension flows away from your body, you will become more and more relaxed, more and more in tune with the natural rhythm of your breathing. (*Pause for 30 seconds*)

Imagine that you are standing by a lake on a lovely spring day. There is still a lingering mist from a brief shower that has just ended, and the sun is beginning to emerge from behind the clouds. The air is clear and still carrying the scent of the spring rain. Looking over the lake, you are startled to see a wonderfully vivid rainbow, appearing out of nowhere to grace the heavens with multicolored splendor: red, green, and blue, with shadings of orange, yellow, and violet. As you gaze in wonder at the beauty, recall the rainbow that appeared at the end of the flood as a sign of God's promise to bless rather than curse the earth, to heal rather than destroy. Looking at the rainbow, let it become for you a sign of promise, God's promise of blessing and healing . . . a rainbow promise of blessing and healing . . . a rainbow promise of blessing and healing . . . a rainbow promise of blessing and healing. (*Pause for 1 minute*)

As if in a dream, imagine yourself transported to the end of the rainbow, a rainbow of blessing and healing that has its origin in heaven and its ending on earth. Imagine all the colors of the rainbow showering on you the blessing and healing that are God's promise to you, a rainbow promise of blessing and healing.

Imagine the rosy-red light of the rainbow glowing around you, surrounding you with soft light . . . seeing it . . . sensing it . . . feeling it as a blessing and healing that God intends for you. Imagine the red light radiating through your skin and into your bloodstream, flowing throughout your body and revitalizing every red and white blood cell, energizing each cell for its task in fighting disease and replenishing food and oxygen to the tissues of your body. (*Pause for 1 minute*)

Imagine the soft green light of the rainbow glowing around you, the beautiful green of the grass and the trees, a green light that is suffused with energy that will enable you to grow into the wholeness that God intends as a blessing for you. Bathing in the green light and drawing from it energy for growing and maintaining wellness . . . feeling the energy flowing throughout your body and revitalizing every cell, bringing harmony and wholeness. (*Pause for 1 minute*)

Imagine that you are surrounded by the color of blue from the rainbow, a shade of blue that matches the color you see in the sky on a perfectly clear and cloudless day, the soft blue light of the rainbow all around you like a garment. Imagine the deep blue light flowing through your eyes and ears into your mind, releasing the energy, inspiration, and wisdom that come as a blessing of God for you. Imagine the blue light swirling through your mind, enabling you to see things more clearly, filling you with the energy to be a force for healing in the world, opening up channels of intuition and insight, and becoming deeply embedded in your inner mind as a wisdom that you can call on at any time. (*Pause for 1 minute*)

As you are ready, slowly and gently return to this room, feeling refreshed and whole in body, mind, and spirit.

The Healing Hands of Christ

Introduction

This exercise was written especially as a meditation for a Lenten service that was part of a series on "The Hands of Lent." Appearing in exactly the form in which it was used, this meditation is an example of how guided imagery can be used in the context of worship. The congregation needs to be given some advance preparation for this type of meditation. The appropriate time for that is at the beginning of the service. I would suggest that the leader of worship introduce the guided meditation in a manner similar to the following:

> There will be a guided meditation instead of the usual homily in our service today. A suggestion will be made at the beginning of the meditation that you either close your eyes or keep them focuesed on the cross. This will keep you from being distracted during the course of the meditation. Let yourself be guided by my words as I focus your attention on the inner world of your experience. Occasionally there will be brief pauses after I have suggested something in particular for you to reflect on. The first part of the meditation will help you relax. When you are fully relaxed, you will discover that your imagination can be a wonderful aid in enriching your meditation on the healing hands of Jesus.

I would urge caution in the use of guided imagery within the liturgy. Most people will welcome its use, and some with great enthusiasm, but there will always be some for whom it will be a hindrance rather than a help. There are some occasions where its use will be particularly appropriate, such as an evening Lenten service with lights dimmed. A guided meditation can be a powerful tool for deepening such an experience. As with all judgments about liturgy, knowledge of the people and the occasion will be the best guide.

Guided Imagery

Listening only to the sound of my voice and either closing your eyes or keeping them focused on the cross so that you can have free access to the world of your imagination and not be distracted by anything around you . . . letting any distracting thoughts that come into your mind float by as if carried away by the wind . . . paying attention only to the natural rhythm of your breathing as you relax in the peace and quiet of this place where God dwells . . . feeling the moving of God's Spirit within you and between you and every other person in this place . . . responding to the call of the Spirit with an inner, intuitive kind of understanding that springs spontaneously from the imagination of faith.

In your mind's eye imagine that you are with Jesus in a quiet, peaceful place, just the two of you. It can be anywhere you choose: a favorite place where you go to be by yourself or some place that you create now in your imagination. Feel the goodness of being there: the beauty of the surroundings, the peace that fills your heart, the calm assurance that you have in the presence of Jesus. Let the busyness of this day, the stress of too much to do and too little time to do it, the problems that are unresolved, let all that fade into the background as you open the chambers of your heart to the indwelling Spirit of God, ready and eager to spend a few moments with Christ the Healer. (*Pause for 30 seconds*)

Concentrate your attention on the hands of Jesus, the healing hands of Jesus that he used so often to touch those whom he healed. What do those hands look like? Are they strong and rugged, like the hands of a carpenter? Or are they smooth and soft, like the hands of an artist? Are they perhaps marked with the print of nails? There are no right or wrong ways to imagine the hands of Jesus. They may look like hands that have held you when you were sick or troubled, such as the hands of your mother or father, the hands of your spouse, or the hands of a good friend. (*Pause for 30 seconds*)

The hands of Jesus are healing hands. Imagine that for eighteen years you have had a back so severely bent that you always have to look at the ground, as was the case with a woman who approached Jesus in the Gospel story. Imagine Jesus putting his hands on your back now as you are bent over — gentle hands, healing hands — and gradually you straighten your back until you can look at Jesus and his healing hands. (*Pause for 15 seconds*)

Imagine that you are blind. If you have your eyes closed, imagine what it would be like if it were that way all of the time, if you had to find your way out of church without being able to see, find your way around your house, wherever you go . . . . . and then Jesus touches your eyes, as he did numerous times with those who were blind, and you are able to see Jesus and his healing hands. (*Pause for 15 seconds*)

In your mind's eye picture your body covered with leprosy: white, scaly scabs and ulcers that are slowly wasting away your skin and causing deformities in your body. Imagine yourself as isolated from others and required to call out "Unclean!" when anyone approached . . . Now feel the touch of Jesus on your skin, the first human touch you have felt for years. As his touch breaks the isolation, it also breaks the grip of the leprosy, and you feel the illness ebb away, like water flowing down the drain. With a grateful heart you look at Jesus and his healing hands. (*Pause for 15 seconds*)

Imagine, if you can, that all life has left your body and that mourners surround the lifeless body that was you. Picture your body as it would be if you had just died . . . . . and then imagine Jesus taking your hand and yourself awakening as if from a dream, like the daughter of Jairus in the Gospels, to see Jesus and his healing hands. (*Pause for 15 seconds*)

Scan your body for any places that hold pain or tension or perhaps illness. Go there with the aid of your imagination and listen very carefully to what your body may have to tell you about the pain or tension that reside there. Symptoms are always messages that our body is sending, but we often don't listen very carefully or listen only when it's like being hit over the head with a baseball bat. Take a moment to listen carefully to what your body may want to tell you. (*Pause for 45 seconds*)

Imagine the healing hands of Jesus pressed firmly but gently at that place in your body that holds pain or tension. Feel the goodness of that touch which is intended for you in order that you might be well. Let the healing energy from his hands penetrate deeply into the muscles and other tissues of your body that are in need of healing. Take a moment to let this experience deepen and to repeat it in any other portion of your body that is in need of healing. (*Pause for 1 minute*)

Picture in your mind's eye the people you know who need the healing hands of Jesus placed on them. Picture them being touched by the healing hands of Jesus inthe same way that he touched the blind, the lepers, and even those who had died. Let this be the form of your prayer for their healing as you imagine each in turn being touched by Jesus. (*Pause for 1 minute*)

Without feeling rushed, come away from your experience of the healing hands of Jesus by opening your eyes and returning to this house of God to continue your worship of our Lord and Healer, who went all the way to the cross that we might be made whole.

Dialogue with Your
Body About Illness and Health

Introduction

The very idea of having a dialogue with your body may seem strange to you. A dialogue between two people is not that difficult to imagine, but most of us tend to think of our body as an object rather than a subject, an "it" rather than a "thou." We often treat our bodies as possessions. We expect them to follow orders no matter how demandng or abusing we are. But we all know from experience that if we push our bodies too hard, they will rebel by refusing to do what we ask and by forcing accommodations on us. Suddenly our bodies are in control and we are the slaves.

Dialogue calls for a different relationship between self and body, a relationship Martin Buber would classify as I-Thou rather than I-It. Giving our bodies the status of persons rather than things requires a different attitude on our part. Rather than being property that we can put to any use we desire, a body–self calls for respect, love, reverence, and even awe. Then it is possible to carry on a dialogue in one's mind between two parties who are ready to listen and willing to change.

A dialogical relationship with one's body is particularly important in periods of illness, because then a feeling of estrangement from one's body is most likely to occur. You take your body for granted in times of relative good health, but it has a way of getting your attention when you are sick. Like the whining of a tired and irritable child, your body's cries of distress are something you cannot ignore. This doesn't mean that you are ready to listen, really listen, to your ailing body any more than you are ready to listen to a whining child. But remarkable things can happen if you can get beyond the irritating demand for attention and reach out to the wounded child underneath, who so desperately needs your understanding and unconditional love.

The following exercise is designed at least to initiate what can become a continuing dialogue with one's body. The exercise appears in two forms, one for use in a group, the other for the spiritual care of a person who is sick. Though both have the same goal, to improve the relationship between self and body, there are some clear differences. It is assumed that those using the exercise in a group setting are relatively healthy, while the spiritual care exercise assumes that the person is sick. Those doing the group experience are encouraged to express themselves in writing, but the sick person will probably prefer to respond orally. The spiritual care setting will be more personal and intimate, allowing the use of touch, and it will call for greater flexibility on the part of the guide.

Some form of preparation for a dialogue with one's body is called for no matter what setting is used. The following paragraph suggests how the exercise might be introduced:

> All too often we treat our bodies as our possessions, to use and misuse as we wish. Scripture speaks of the body as having a dignity equal to that of the self, both being expressions of yourself as a person. As a gift from God, your body is sacred and to be treated with the respect that belongs to the "temple of the Holy Spirit" (1 Cor. 6:19). The voice of our body can be a vehicle for the voice of God. To give your body such a voice is the purpose of the dialogue that follows.

EXERCISE 1, WITHIN A GROUP SETTING

Guided Imagery

> Let your body relax and sink into the chair you are sitting on . . . letting your eyes close or keeping them focused on one particular spot in order not to be distracted by me or anything going on outside you . . . letting the sound of my voice guide you gently into the center of your inner being . . . attuning yourself to the world within rather than the world outside . . . becoming aware of your breathing as the natural rhythm of your body . . . breathing in . . . and breathing out . . . moving ever deeper to the center of your inner being . . . listening to the voice of your body

. . . letting all the voices that have been demanding your attention fade into the background until they are no more than distant echoes. (*Pause for 20 seconds*)

As you move more and more deeply into the region of your inner self, become aware of seeing your body from within rather than looking at your body as if it were some external object, like when you look in the mirror. Become aware of your body from within, your breathing in and out in a natural, regular rhythm. Scan different parts of your body for any tension that might be there, and then release that tension so that your body can feel relaxed and at ease. Pay attention to what your body is telling you about its needs: perhaps the need for nourishment . . . or for rest . . . or for exercise . . . or for touch. (*Pause for 30 seconds*) Are you surprised at either the number or the intensity of the needs? Do those needs seem legitimate to you? What has kept you from meeting those needs? (*Pause for 1 minute*)

The body that is you had its beginning long before you were aware of becoming a person. Return with the aid of your imagination to the beginning of your body. Since you can do anything that you want with your imagination, imagine that your beginning was like Adam's, God forming your body out of the dust of the ground to be absolutely unique, unlike anybody else who has ever lived. Imagine that as God breathes into you the breath of life, your whole body suddenly becomes alive and fully functioning. Imagine your breath to be God's breath within you, your breathing in tune with the rhythm of the universe. (*Pause for 30 seconds*)

Your body, for all the wonder of its created goodness, has been formed from the earth and will return to the earth, as subject to pain, suffering, and loss as every other earth creature. Let your body tell you the story of its woundedness from the beginning until now. Let your mind drift back over the years, and as you recall events of trauma to your body, record them on the paper in front of you with a word or phrase. The wound may have been a broken arm or leg, or it may have been a long or a short illness. The trauma may have been widespread throughout your body or localized in one place. It may have been on the surface for all to see or hidden deep inside. The trauma may have come and gone, or it may have left a wound that will never heal or a space that will never be filled. Take a moment to scan your body-memory and then list on the left-hand side of the paper the injuries and illnesses that you recall in whatever order they come to you. (*Pause for 2 minutes*)

After you have completed the list, redo the sequence of items in the order of their importance: important for the lesson it taught you or for its lasting impact or because the wound is fresh and frightening. Let your judgments be spontaneous, flowing out of the story of your body. (*Pause for 1 minute*)

With a deeper awareness of your body and its woundedness, you are ready for a dialogue with your body about illness and injury. Sitting in quietness with your eyes closed . . . focusing your attention inward . . . become aware of the presence of your body as a person, a person with a story to tell, a person with needs and fears and hopes. As you feel the presence of your body as a person grow stronger within you, you may be aware of an image of your body taking shape within your imagination: perhaps in the form of a person who bears the marks of many wounds on his or her body or in the form of a wise old man or woman. If such an image appears to your mind's eye, you may want to give the person a name in order that the dialogue may flow more smoothly. If not, simply be aware of your body as a presence within you. (*Pause for 30 seconds*)

Remaining in quietness with your eyes closed, let the presence of your body as a person grow stronger. As you feel ready, greet the person who is your body and listen closely to what your body has to say about the wounds your body has suffered over the years, the threats of illness and injury in the past. Go back to each of the traumas you listed to refresh your body-memory about those wounds, asking about their meaning and what they have taught you. Listen to what your body needs from you in the future, especially in facing the trauma that will be the end of the story of your body. Let the dialogue script between you and your body flow freely, recordng both what you say and what your body-self says, your pen simply recording what is there without censoring or interpreting. Let the inner dialogue proceed in silence. (*Allow 10–15 minutes for writing*)

EXERCISE 2, FOR THE SPIRITUAL CARE OF THE SICK

Introduction

The most frequent use of this exercise will likely be by individuals for spiritual self-care. It is well suited for that purpose, especially if your attention span is limited, and you are looking for a relatively short exercise.

If you are using this exercise as a spiritual care guide, I suggest that you remain as flexible as possible in directing the guided imagery process. Much will depend on the personality, experience, capacity for imagery, and type and stage of illness of the person doing the exercise. The guide should have a map of the journey in mind, as well as a destination, but be ready to follow a number of different routes to get there, depending on the variables just mentioned. The exercise as written is one such map, which has as its goal the linking of the experience of the body as ill with the experience of the body as the temple of the Holy Spirit.

Guided Imagery

Let your body relax and feel at ease to the extent that this is possible in your present state of illness . . . letting your eyes close as your body relaxes . . . letting the sound of my voice guide you gently inside your body awareness . . . attuning yourself to the world inside rather than the world outside . . . becoming aware of your breathing as the natural rhythm of your body . . . moving deeper into the center of your inner being in order to listen to the voice of your body . . . paying attention only to the sound of my voice and the voice of your own body.

As you move more and more deeply into the region of your inner self, become awre of seeing your body from within rather than looking at your body as if it were some external object, like when you look in a mirror. As you become aware of your body from within, pay attention to your breathing, breathing in and out in a natural, regular rhythm. Your breathing is you. Feel a unity with your breathing. Feel a unity with your body.

Your body is a special creation of God. In order for you to have a deeper sense of that, go all the way back to the origins of your body-self, long before you had the capacity even to be aware of your body. Imagine that your beginning was like Adam's, God forming your body out of the dust of the ground to be absolutely unique, unlike anybody else who has ever lived. Imagine God breathing into you the breath of life so that your breath is God's breath, your breathing in tune with the rhythm of the universe, your being in the image of God.

Saint Paul calls the human body a temple of the Holy Spirit, a sacred place. Other images can convey the same sense of holiness: a body filled with light that radiates outward, a body so filled with the Spirit of God that there is a tongue of fire on the head, a body with a face that glows with an inner light, a body with a halo surrounding it. Choose an image that fits with your felt sense of being filled with the Holy Spirit. (*Pause for 30 seconds*) Tell me when you've found an image that seems right. Describe the image for me. If the image seems external to you, then step into that image right now so that you and your body are one and filled with the Holy Spirit. (*Pause for 15 seconds*)

With the aid of your imagination, go to the place within your body where it feels the worst right now, the place within your body that is bearing the burden of the illness. Simply be aware of the pain or whatever it is that feels wrong. (*Pause for 30 seconds*) Perhaps an image will form that will express how this feels, or maybe you will be aware of something that your body is trying to say that you haven't been hearing because other things have been demanding your attention. Don't try to force anything. Simply be aware of what is there. (*Pause for 1 minute*) What have you been experiencing? Is there anything that surprises you? (*Pause for 30 seconds*)

Return to the image you had before of your body as sacred, as filled with the Holy Spirit. Bring that image to the place within your body that is bearing the burden of your illness. If it's hard to unite your body as sacred with your body as sick, then imagine them side by side in two different chairs. What would they say to each other? Let your sick body speak first, and then let your sacred body answer. (*Pause for 1 minute*)

(*Bring the exercise to a close with a prayer that flows out of the imagery experience, and encourage the person to record the dialogue in writing if he or she feels strong enough.*)

Spiritual Healing Exercise

Introduction

The following exercise is for general use, either with a group or an individual. If used in providing spiritual care to a person who is sick, there can be considerable dialogue during the course of the exercise. You may want to add a ritual similar to the ancient practice of the laying on of hands. After the person has identified some portion of his or her body where there is tension and a sense of imbalance, place your hand or hands at that place and say, "Imagine that my hands are the hands of Christ the Healer." This is no mere stretch of the imagination, since our hands are the hands of the body of Christ and can convey his healing touch.

Not everyone will be able to visualize the Spirit of Christ within them, as this exercise directs them to do, either because light or energy is not the best image for them or because no images at all seem to work. Talk about this at the beginning of the exercise in order to give the persons doing the exercise the permission to substitute imagery of their own when that seems appropriate and to assure them that the exercise will work just as well if they have a sense of the presence of Christ without any visual image.

Guided Imagery

Imagine that the chair you are sitting on is a recliner, and you are able to sink into it with great comfort . . . relaxing into the music and listening only to my words as I guide you to a quiet place inside yourself . . . letting all other sounds that you may hear and all other distracting thoughts that may come into your mind fade into the background . . . knowing that this exercise for spiritual healing is the most important thing that you have to do right now . . . becoming aware of your breathing in its smooth and natural rhythm . . . always in perfect harmony with the rest of your body . . . breathing in the breath of life, the breath that

God first breathed into Adam . . . breathing in the Spirit of God, who brings healing into your life . . . breathing out fear and anything that keeps you from fully being the child of God that you are . . . sitting in quiet and calm . . . aware only of the sound of my voice and the gentle movement of your breathing, breathing that brings peace and quiet and readiness for healing . . . waiting calmly with quiet hope for the movement of the Spirit of God deep within you . . . aware of seeing things as you've never seen them before, of hearing with more than your ear, of knowing with more than your mind.

As the stillness deepens within you, imagine that you are on a path in a forest that is familiar to you. The trees are tall, forming a huge canopy of overlapping branches that act as a ceiling to cover you. The bright sun above filters through the branches, sending little rays to dot the forest path with patches of light. The path is leading to a place of peace and comfort. You have walked on this path before. It leads to a place where you are free to be the person that God created you to be. As you walk, listen to the sounds around you . . . smell the freshness . . . see the beauty of the cathedral-like forest . . . feel the wind gently brushing your cheek . . . sense how lightly and easily your body moves. Feel the presence of the Spirit of God in this place, a presence that is not only in the forest but in you, filling you with love and energy and healing. Take a moment to continue your walk along this familiar path to a place deep within you where the Spirit of God dwells. (*Pause for 1 minute*)

As the stillness deepens, envision the Spirit of God within you as the Spirit of Christ the Healer. Listen closely to his soft voice whispering in you ear, "God wants you to be whole in body, mind, and spirit, to be balanced and harmonious in every dimension of your being." Imagine the Spirit of Christ filling your entire being in any way that seems right: as light, as energy, as a sense of power or presence . . . bringing healing where there is disease, peace where there is discord, hope where there is despair, forgiveness where there is guilt, joy where there is discouragement. (*Pause for 30 seconds*)

Imagine the Spirit of Christ moving through every corner of your body: discerning where there is imbalance, where your body is holding conflict, where there is un-resolved tension. With your mind's eye go to the area that seems most seriously out of balance. Let an image form of what your body is holding there. It may be a realistic image of what that part of your body looks like and what is wrong with it. Or it may be a more fanciful picture, like a vise causing pressure or a rope with a tight knot in it. Take a moment to let the image form in a way that feels right to you. (*Pause for 1 minute*)

Bring the Spirit of Christ to that place in your body where you are most conscious of distress and imbalance. Listen to the voice of Jesus asking, "Do you want to be healed?" Listen carefully to your response, especially to any resistance to change. Let an image form in your mind of what is taking place as you sense the presence of Christ's Spirit where you feel tension and discord. Again you hear the question, "Do you want to be healed?" Pay attention to your response. Watching . . . listening . . . feeling what is hap-pening. (*Pause for 30 seconds*)

Now hear the words "Your faith has made you well. . . Go in peace." Let the healing presence of Christ work within you . . . noticing how God's healing power spreads through your body . . . feeling an energy from beyond you filling your whole being. (*Pause for 30 seconds*) Resting quietly now as the healing process continues. (*Pause for 2 minutes*)

As you are ready, gently bring yourself back to this room, feeling refreshed, healed, and ready to use your health and wholeness in the service of God and those in need of your healing presence.

Healing the Wounded Child Within

Introduction

Much has been written in the last few years about healing the inner child. It has been used in both spiritual care and secular therapy as an effective way to help people come to terms with painful memories from their past. The purpose of the following exercise is to bring the wounded child within to Christ for the healing that only his presence can bring.

For those who are not familiar with the metaphor of the inner child, it refers to past experiences that were painful. It may have been a cherished relationship that became strained, even broken. It may have been some personal tragedy, like the loss of a job or the death of someone you loved and needed very much. It may have been some terrible wrong done to you or inflicted by you. Whatever the incident, it left you wounded. Sometimes the wound is so deep that it remains open and festering for years. Sometimes a scar has formed, but another trauma or some close association with the original trauma opens the wound all over again. In any case, the healing is not complete, and the wound needs tending.

Developmental psychologists tell us that we grow in layers, meaning that earlier stages of development remain in place within the deeper levels of our consciousness. Thus it makes sense to speak of an inner child, a child who was wounded and continues to feel the pain for a long time. In order to protect ourselves from dealing with the pain, we isolate the child within and act as if the wound had never been inflicted or that it has completely healed. The inner child knows better but has no voice. The metaphor of child also captures the sense of vulnerability and neediness that is associated with such experiences. It is cruel to treat the child within you or within someone else as if she or he were grown up. When you are very little, you need protection and nurture, not a lecture on being responsible and acting like a grown-up.

Does the child who has been wounded need to forgive the person who inflicted the wound in order to be healed? The literature on this subject often suggests that to be the case. Reconciliation brings healing, of course. But forgiving a hurt that has been inflicted by another, especially a deep wound from early in life, is not always possible and should never be expected. It's not enough to say that one should not be forced into granting forgiveness until ready to do so spontaneously. The implication is that at some point the readiness will be there, or at least ought to be. But an adult who was abused as a child, for instance, is likely to have a wound so deep that forgiving the abuser would be nothing less than miraculous.

This exercise can be done with a group, because everybody has inner hurts, but it can be particularly effective in providing spiritual care to a person who is aware of a long-standing wound. One can also do this as an exercise in self-care, although the warmth and acceptance that comes from another person caring for you will be lacking. For some people the privacy of their inner world is the only safe environment for making contact with the wounded child who resides there.

Guided Imagery

Take several deep breaths and exhale slowly, and as you exhale feel yourself relax as all tension and stress is released . . . breathing in . . . and slowly breathing out . . . breathing in . . . and slowly breathing out . . . feeling more and more relaxed . . . letting all distracting thoughts float out of your consciousness like clouds drifting over the horizon . . . letting your breathing come more slowly and evenly . . . moving gradually and easily on a downward path to the center of your self . . . letting the sound of my voice and any other sound that you hear take you deeper into the inner world of your experience.

Imagine a room deep within the world of your inner experience that is reserved for you and you alone. You can furnish that room however you wish, knowing that the room is only for you, and nobody else will be allowed to enter. Picture yourself in that room now, perhaps on a recliner and gazing reflectively at a fire burning brightly in a fireplace, and with soft music playing in the background. You can feel perfectly safe here to explore any memory, any fantasy, any feeling, any thought. You have time to be alone with yourself and your inner thoughts and feelings without fear of being exposed or judged. Take a moment to let the experience deepen of being safe and secure in a room deep within the world of your inner experience. (*Pause for 30 seconds*)

From within the safety and security of this special room, imagine that you are floating down the stream of your life. Imagine yourself entering that stream at the point of your earliest memories, and then floating safely and slowly past all of the events and experiences that are stored in your memory. Pay attention to the experiences that evoke feelings of pain as you come upon them. As you recall painful memories, note them with a word or phrase on the paper before you. Without dwelling on the pain, continue your journey down the stream of your life, and note other events and experiences that are painful to remember. You may be surprised at memories long forgotten. Simply note them and continue your journey. I will give you sufficient time to complete that journey. (*Pause for 20 minutes*)

Opening your eyes just enough to scan the list of memories that you have noted, choose the one that you would like to explore further, either because you are aware that it comes from a deep and long-standing wound or because it seems to be in particular need of your attention at this time. (*Pause for 20 seconds*)

Very tenderly and gently reenter that painful memory. Give yourself permission to feel the pain that is evoked as you reenter that experience. Picture a wounded child coming out of the hurt that you feel, a child who is very timid and very needy. Take the hand of this wounded child and lead her or him to a lovely meadow where Jesus is sitting, surrounded by a group of children who are eagerly listening to a story he is telling them. Be aware of any resistance on the part of the wounded child to joining the group. Perhaps it's a fear of being exposed or a feeling of unworthiness or a fear of needing too much. (*Pause for 20 seconds*)

Imagine Jesus looking up and seeing the needy child you have been leading to him. Picture Jesus leaving the other children, walking over to the wounded child, taking the child in his arms, and holding her or him in his lap. Look at the expression on the faces of Jesus and the needy child. Listen carefully to what the child tells Jesus and to what Jesus says in return. I'll give you a moment to let that experience unfold naturally and spontaneously within you. (*Pause for 1 minute*)

Now imagine Jesus turning to you and talking to you about the wounded child he has been comforting. Listen carefully to what he has to say about the neediness of this child, about the vulnerability of being very little and not able to handle things like a grown-up, about how much this wounded child needs to be loved and accepted in order to be healed. If you can, imagine yourself taking this wounded child into your arms and simply holding her or him without saying anything or trying to make it all better. If that doesn't feel right, don't force it; leave the wounded child in the arms of Jesus, and perhaps another time you might be ready to hold the child. (*Pause for 30 seconds*) As the experience deepens and you feel ready, begin a conversation between you and the wounded child within you. Record that conversation in writing, both what the child says and what you say. Let that conversation flow easily and naturally, expressing openly and honestly the fears and the needs that you both have. (*Allow 5–10 minutes for writing*)

Appendix

The Use of Imagery in the
Healing Ministry of the Church

Even a cursory reading of the Gospels makes it clear that healing was a vital part of the ministry of Jesus, so much so that he has been called the Great Physician and Christ the Healer. The sharp distinctions we make between *save* and *heal* are absent from the healing stories of Jesus. In the story of the healing of the paralytic in Mark 2, Jesus forgives when he is expected to heal and heals when he is expected to forgive. Healing and saving are aspects of a larger whole, the care of the whole person. The healing stories of Jesus make it abundantly clear that his intention is the mending of all creation, which means healing the body as well as saving the soul. He would no more have told the sick that he could not heal them because it was the will of God that they be sick than parents would tell their children that they could not feed them because it was the will of God that they be hungry.

That Jesus intended healing to be as central to the church's ministry as it was to his is clear from accounts of Jesus sending his disciples, on one occasion twelve and another seventy, on misionary journeys (Luke 9 and 10). In both, Jesus gives two commands, to preach and to heal. The mission of the church is the mending of creation and spreading the good news about what God is doing in the world to save (heal) it. And the disciples take that commission seriously. Many healings are recorded in the Acts of the Apostles and the writings of the church fathers. In fact, there never has been a time when healing was not part of the church's tradition.

The history of the church's tradition of healing is check-
ered. Many bright moments reflect both the spirit and practice of Christ the Healer, but dark moments cloud and
sometimes distort his vision of a healing church. Some of
the bright moments: the building and staffing of hospitals,
among the first in the West; the development of sacramental
rituals of healing; the ministry of responsible charismatic
healers; the ministry of medical missions. Some of the dark
moments: spawning magical notions of healing based on
superstition rather than faith; narrowing the healing ministry of the church to the salvation of the soul; using the
authority of the church to limit and even forbid the practice
of medicine. However one judges this past, and I see it as
more positive than negative. Healing is of the essence of the
church, not just a good thing to do but integral to what it
means to be the church.

Currently there is a renewal of interest in the healing
ministry of the church. A variety of factors have contributed to this renewal. One is an emphasis on the whole person in health care. For centuries both medicine and religion
have agreed to a division between soul and body that has
allowed each its own area of expertise. Both sides agree that
this distinction no longer holds. Holistic and behavioral
medicine are representative of a general shift away from the
purely objective and mechanistic approach of traditional
medical science; healing services wellness programs, and
innovations like the parish nurse program are representative of a much broader concern for the whole person in
the church.

Spirituality and Health

A distinction between physical care (medicine) and spiritual
care (religion) is still needed, of course. The term *spirituality*
has gained favor in Christian circles in recent years, replac-
ing terms descriptive of religious experience that have
negative connotations, such as *piety* and *holiness*. The term
spiritual healing would seem to be the logical choice for
designating the religious approach to whole-person health
care, but it has associations with earlier usages that make
the choice questionable. In the past, spiritual healing has

meant miracle cure, a supernatural intervention by God that was as much an act by an external agent as an intervention by medical science. Spiritual healing has also been closely associated with Christian Science, where it refers exclusively to the healing of the mind or spirit with no reference at all to the body.

Though the term *spiritual healing* is colored by the beliefs of Christian Science and miracle cures, it is still the best choice of a parallel term to physical healing. Spiritual healing is healing of the whole person via the human spirit, which includes such things as attitude, meaning making, and expectant trust. Healing via the human spirit is as concrete and natural as physical healing but much more complex and difficult to verify. Spiritual healing covers phenomena like the placebo effect, which refers to the healing power of expectant trust. Spiritual healing focuses on the meaning of illness, about which one can learn only by going beyond the traditional case history of a patient and inquiring into the story of illness. Spiritual healing is the best choice of terms for describing the effects of using imagery in healing, now widespread in the field of medicine and deserving greater use in religion, where it nurtures the spirituality that gives it healing power.

The church can make a major contribution to whole-person health care in this broad area of spirituality and health. This is not to say that spirituality and health is the exclusive province of religion (that would repeat the error of past controversies, but spirituality is more naturally situated in the realm of religion. And not just religion in general. Spirituality is nurtured in a faith tradition, even though that may be more implicit than explicit. Stated differently, spirituality is never without content. If the spirituality is expectant trust, then it's trust in someone or something. If the spirituality is the meaning of illness, then the story of illness will enable us to discern the faith by which this person lives. If the spirituality is the use of imagery for healing, then it is a matter of analyzing the content of the imagery and the context in which it is done for the faith that gives it meaning.

There is not much in Western culture or most of Christianity that either motivates or trains people for the use of imagery. Indeed, we are warned against it by both science and Christian orthodoxy. The irony is that the very objectivity of science and Christian orthodoxy has given rise to a deep hunger for spirituality among Christians in the West. Unfortunately, most people do not perceive the church as a place where their hunger for spirituality can be satisfied. In a 1978 Gallup poll, 60 percent of churchgoers agreed with the statement "Most churches have lost the real spiritual part of religion." Judging by the attraction of Eastern religions and New Age phenomena in this country, many people yearn for an inner religious experience. A recent study showed that the majority of respondents thought that getting to know the inner self was more important than a high-paying job, having a beautiful home, or belonging to a church or synagogue. What many people are looking for in religion but not finding in churches is an experience of a richer and deeper reality than what we are aware of with the limited tools of analysis and critique that we normally use to interpret the world around us. Imagery is a mode of whole knowing that probes and gives expression to this deeper level of reality in the inner world of our experience.

I believe that imagery can facilitate healing and that it should be grounded in a specific faith tradition, in this case the Christian faith. Your interest in healing imagery is an indication that you either share those assumptions or are willing to test them. It might be helpful, however, to look at some of the reason for resistance to the use of imagery.

Resistance to the Use of Imagery Among Christians

Many Christians are not so much resistant to the use of imagery as they are unaware of it and the world of inner experience that it explores. I am regularly asked to explain guided imagery to people who have never heard of it or who have misconceptions about it. Some Christians are somewhat suspicious of the use of imagery, mostly because of its association with the New Age movement and the power of positive thinking. In churches where I tested the guided imagery exercises in this volume, I was consistently asked: How does this differ from New Age imagery? Is this the same thing that Norman Cousins and Bernie Siegel are advocating? There was both curiosity and some suspicion in these questions, but no hostility. For others, however, the use of imagery is a highly charged issue and treated with open hostility. Authors like Douglas Groothius and Constance Cumbey link New Age imagery with Satanism and warn readers against any use of imagery. What are the roots of this suspicion and hostility?

Protestants tend to be suspicious of mysticism in particular and interiority in general. This is not to say that Catholics are unaware of the dangers of exploring the inner world. One of the best known of the mystics, Saint Teresa, of Avila warned that "the imagination (the fool of the house) romps and frolics wildly where it wishes." The goal of medieval mystics was to move beyond the illuminative stage (meditation on images) to the unitive stage (an imageless union with God). However, awareness of the shadow side of the inner world did not deter the mystics from their quest for inner enlightenment.

By contrast, some Protestants are opposed to mystical experience on doctrinal grounds. The twin doctrines of deep human sinfulness and justification by grace are at the core of this opposition. A journey inward is a journey into the domain of sin that so easily misguides us. Only the gracious action of God can free us from the sinful condition of our total humanity. Explore the uncharted and dangerous world of your inner experience only at the risk of your soul's salvation.

Emphasis on an objective gospel that has validity and authority because of what God alone could do leaves little or no room for faith as experience. Luther argued that faith is a gift of God and in no way an act of the person. Thus taking your spiritual pulse all of the time is having "faith in faith." Luther's attitude is typical of a general suspicion in Protestantism of any spirituality that focuses on inner experience, especially if it is an unmediated mystical experience of God. Word and sacrament are the means of grace, these alone, and they are external to the self and all of the ambiguities and distortions of inner experience.

There are reasons for resistance to the use of imagery other than suspicion of inner subjective experience. One is pride, which can lead a person who has had a profound spiritual experience to assume a position of superiority to those who haven't. Second, there is always the danger of pathology. Calling up images out of the deepest recesses of your inner being is opening yourself to the worst as well as the best that is within. You may not meet Satan within, but how about the neurotic and phobic fantasies that sometimes haunt our dreams? However devout our intentions, our spirituality is not exempt from these forces. Finally, caution about unstructured interior reflection is in order because of the risk of distortion. Symbols of faith are generated and nurtured by the creative imagination, but so are distortions of those symbols.

Overcoming Resistance to the Use of Imagery

Resistance to the use of imagery should be regarded as negative only when, like an entrenched defense mechanism, it becomes so rigid that it stifles the hunger for a spirituality that deepens the experience of faith. Is there imagery that can satisfy this hunger while avoiding the dangers that prompt resistance to it?

Drawing images directly from Scripture is a safeguard against a spirituality of healing that is either self-grounded or grounded in some promise other than that of the gospel. The value of a biblically based imagery is that it can remain faithful to Scripture while deepening the experience of those who are encountering God through the text. Imagery should be subjected to the same scrutiny as preaching or any other form of witness to the gospel to ensure its faithfulness to the norm of Scripture. To condemn the use of imagery because the form of communication is different from the linear, logical mode of verbal discourse is to miss the purpose of reflecting on Scripture and to ignore the mode of communication that characterizes so much of its witness.

Images abound in the stories, parables, and metaphors of Scripture. These images can evoke and express faith much more profoundly than doctrine. The image of Jesus as the good shepherd does more to strengthen faith than the most sophisticated theological argument for the providence of God. The images of cross and empty tomb are more expressive of the gospel than a clear and coherent formulation of the doctrine of justification by grace through faith. The liturgy, with its heavy use of symbols and ritual actions, is closer to imagery than abstract confessional formulas. Preaching is enhanced by the use of images in stories that make faith come alive. The sacramental life of the church is enriched by images like "heavenly banquet" and "body of Christ." In the same way imagery can deepen and strengthen the faith of God's people in the promise of healing.

Ira Progoff once told of writing in his journal, "Suppose the Nazis had burned all the Bibles in the world. What would happen? . . . Well, we'd just have to make new ones from the same place that the old ones were made." Progoff is not talking about the memory of the Christian community but symbols coming out of the collective unconscious. This will not do. For Christians, word and sacrament provide the structure for the inward journey. They keep us in touch with the God of history who acts in our history through these means of grace. It is important to understand that one takes the inner journey in order to enhance word and sacrament, not to replace them.

Most of us are not likely to err on the side of moving too deeply into the inner world of our experience and there getting lost in pathologies or distortions of the true meaning of Christianity. We are much more likely to err on the side of too much caution, too much resistance. Trust the spirituality that has been nurtured in you through word and sacrament, and that will serve as a reliable guide in any journey that you take into the inner world of your experience. Take the plunge into deeper waters and use the feedback of fellow members in the body of Christ to help you reflect on the meaning of your experience.

The Use of Imagery in Giving Expression to Bodily Spirituality

We have become alienated from our bodies. The higher we go in social status, the more alienated we become. The myth of a society is expressed through the body. Those at the highest echelons never get dirty, never sweat, never touch anyone, and rarely use their bodies in an active way. Technology has freed most people from manual labor, including those who work in industry. The machine has become a model of life and a metaphor of body.

The traditional biomedical model reinforces that way of thinking about the body, treating the body like a machine in need of repair, diagnosing the prblems objectively like a mechanic, and prescribing treatment that will put the body back in working order. If we think of our bodies as machines, then it's no wonder we're angry when they break down. It's like any other piece of property that we own. We expect good performance and feel let down if it doesn't work well.

The sense of alienation from our bodies is aggravated by a theology that depicts the body as evil and a source of continual temptation. When Saint Paul talks about the conflict between flesh and spirit, he's referring to the alienation of the whole person from the Spirit of God, but most people regard sins of the flesh as sins of the body. If the body is regarded as the primary source of temptation in one's life, then control, if not subjugation, is what will inform the spirituality of the body.

A Christian understanding of health and healing suggests a different kind of spirituality of the body. Health is wholeness of body and spirit. Healing is getting in touch with the natural rhythms of the body. Women are generally closer to their bodies than men, partly because of the menstrual cycle and giving birth, and partly because their life-style until recently has not been as abusive to their bodies as the life-style of men (high stress, heavy smoking, hard driving). Women also have a clearer sense that wholeness is relatedness, being a part. It has been my experience that women find it easier and more natural to do imagery than men. They are more in tune with their bodies and more willing to allow the body to express spontaneously the feelings that reside there.

What we need is a spirituality of the body. Because imagery is the language of the body, it is a prime resource for giving expression to the body, for "letting the body pray," as Flora Wuellner puts it (*Prayer and Our Bodies*). Breathing can be an act of praying if one concentrates on the deeper level of the activity, which is the sacramental dimension of breathing that heightens awareness of the presence of God both in and beyond our bodies. Inspiration is a term that comes from the image of God's breathing into us—quite literally in the description of Adam's enlivening and more figuratively in the description of those who wrote the sacred Scriptures. Every breath that we inhale is an occasion for reflection on the life of God within us.

In conclusion, a warning is in order against a preoccupation with one's own need for healing. Healing imagery is appealing to the self-serving narcissism in us all. When this attitude creeps into the church as a motivation for healing prayer, the danger of misusing imagery is high: "I am in need of healing. God has the power to heal. Imagery is a ritual for gaining access to that power."

Prayer, including prayer for healing, should be in tune with what God intends for us and for the world, not what we want from God and from the world for ourselves. The Gospels do not keep us guessing about what Jesus intended for those who came to him for healing; he intended for them to be whole in body, mind, and spirit. But wholeness includes holiness. Those who are healed become healers. Those who are loved become lovers. Health, in the sense of individual wellness, is always a means to an end, never an end in itself.

The faith that heals is both expectant trust, receiving the gift of healing from God, and commitment, giving oneself in service to the cause of healing others and the world. The trust of faith must always be complemented by commitment to the way of the cross, the way of the Wounded Healer.